# IN THE
# TRADITION
# OF
# MOSES
# AND
# MOHAMMED

# IN THE TRADITION OF MOSES AND MOHAMMED

## Jewish and Arab Folktales

Blanche L. Serwer-Bernstein

JASON ARONSON INC.
*Northvale, New Jersey*
*London*

The design of this book is the creation of the staff at Jason Aronson Inc.

This book was set in 11 pt. Bookman by Alpha Graphics of Pittsfield, New Hampshire, and printed by Haddon Craftsmen in Scranton, Pennsylvania.

Copyright © 1994 by Blanche L. Serwer-Bernstein

**Library of Congress Cataloging-in-Publication Data**

Serwer-Bernstein, Blanche, 1920–
    In the tradition of Moses and Mohammed : Jewish and Arab folktales / Blanche L. Serwer-Bernstein.
        p.   cm.

    1. Jews—Folklore.   2. Tales—Israel.   3. Arabs—Folklore.
    4. Tales—Arab countries.   I. Title.
    GR98.S43   1994
    398.2'089924—dc20                                        93-29375

Manufactured in the United States of America. Jason Aronson Inc. offers books and cassettes. For information and catalog write to Jason Aronson Inc., 230 Livingston Street, Northvale, New Jersey 07647.

To my grandchildren,
Zachary, Tammy, Jared, Rebecca, and Adam,
With love and appreciation
For who they are

# CONTENTS

**Folktales Told by Immigrants to Israel
after World War II: Folk Festival in Sedot Mikhah**

**PART II**
**ARAB TALES**

# ACKNOWLEDGMENTS

I started so early in life to enjoy Jewish folktales that I must attribute this interest to the influence of my parents and my childhood home. There I encountered the Golem, the foolish Chelmites, the witches of Ascalon, King Solomon, and the others who populate the first segment of this book. In my childhood fantasies, my telling of the stories would be more vivid than the folklore versions I had read or heard.

I am grateful for the opportunity I had to continue my interest in Jewish literature and folklore as a student at the Teachers' Institute of the Jewish Theological Seminary, where I received a BHL degree in Hebrew literature. During the same four years, I had the wonderful opportunity to pursue my secular studies at Barnard College, where I earned my BA in English literature. I extend to both these great institutions of learning my gratitude for the four productive years I spent on the upper end of Broadway.

I attribute to Harvard University's creative faculty and the library committee of the School of Education the inspiration to write the first group of stories, which had been in my head for a long time. These tales appeared in a small volume entitled *Let's Steal the Moon*, which targeted children as its readers but included college students among its most enthusiastic fans.

I extend my thanks to Boston University for the opportunity, during my professorship there, to teach at Oranim, the *kibbutz* training school for psychologists. While in Israel I received a phone call from Dr. Dov Noy, Grunwald Professor of folklore and literature at the Hebrew University, inviting me to meet his students in Jerusalem. For my continued pursuit of Jewish stories, I am indebted to Dr. Noy. I was easy prey to his contagious love of Jewish folklore and his understanding of its importance in the preservation of Jewish continuity.

What I appreciate most in Dov Noy is his generosity in granting me the opportunity to browse in the folklore archives and to use the stories in my own way. In making the Israel Folk Archives (IFA) available to me as he did to others, he allowed me the freedom of "listening" to Jewish storytellers from around the world, of choosing the tales I loved, and of telling them in my own fashion in the second segment of this book.

Naturally I asked Professor Noy to write introductions to the Jewish segments. He graciously agreed, and his scholarly approach to folktales is now an intrinsic part of this volume. His informative prefaces are here for you to read and enjoy.

For my interest in Arab tales, I wish to acknowledge the colorful imagination of the ancestors of the Arab people who were living side by side with Jews during the thirties when I first visited Palestine. Thanks to the Hebrew University library in Jerusalem, to the Harvard library in Cambridge, and to the Forty-second Street library in New York, I was able to read hundreds of Arabic folktales. Finally, I selected the stories included in this volume, several of them subsumed under the rubric of two medleys.

I am grateful to Dr. Hasan El-Shamy, professor of folklore at Indiana University and at its Arab Institute, for his graciousness in reading the Arab tales and in writing his foreword to the Arab segment. His praise for my versions of the stories encouraged me to shed my doubts about my ability to do with Arab folktales what I had done with Jewish stories.

I am indebted to the Oxford University Press for the quotations from the Bible, which I excerpted from the Authorized King James version of *The Holy Bible.*

For the quotation from the Koran, I am grateful to Dr. Mohammed Salem Agwa, director of the Islamic Center located in New York City.

For the accuracy of the history covered in the introduction, I acknowledge the two books I used to check the facts as I remembered them: *A History of the Arab Peoples* by Albert Habib Hourani, published in 1991 by Belknap Press of the Harvard University Press, and *Jews, God and History* by Max I. Dimont, published in 1962 by Simon and Schuster.

For the Hillel tale of the bluebird and the worm, I thank the publishers of *Lost Legends of Israel* by Dagobert Runes, included in the Philosophical Library of New York, 1961.

I extend my gratitude to Arthur Kurzweil, my editor and vice president of Jason Aronson, who encouraged me throughout the many months of writing and organizing the stories, the introduction, and the forewords; to Muriel Jorgensen, director of editorial production; and to Janet Warner, production editor.

I especially want to thank Loriece Griffiths for her help in the time-consuming process of careful proofreading.

The fans rooting for me on the sidelines of this complicated and time-consuming endeavor were my three sons and their wives, Philip and Ellen G. Serwer, Daniel P. and Jacquelyn D. Serwer, and Jeremy R. and Nancy C. Serwer. I appreciate their patience with my enthusiasm for the project.

And he shall judge among the nations, and shall rebuke many people: and they shall beat their swords into plowshares, and their spears into pruninghooks: nation shall not lift up sword against nation, neither shall they learn war any more.

Isaiah 2:4

But every enemy inclines toward peace. Do thou also incline toward peace, and trust in Allah, for he is the one that hears and knows all things.

The Koran, Surah 8:61

To every thing there is a season, and a time to every purpose under
the heaven:
A time to kill, and a time to heal; a time to break down and a
time to build up;
A time to get, and a time to lose; a time to keep, and a time to
cast away;
A time to love, and a time to hate; a time of war, and a time of
peace.

Ecclesiastes 3:1, 3, 6, 8

# INTRODUCTION

## COEXISTENCE

*Coexistence of the Tales in This Book*

In my fantasy this book is a metaphor for coexistence. The tales of Arabs and Jews rest peaceably together within its covers.

The two sets of stories are quite different in countless ways: tempo, imagery, customs, humor, and what might be called "background music." Yet the two peoples, whose imagination and creativity gave us the tales, are both laying claim to the land of the Bible. And both have a common history of remarkable coexistence in Spain during a golden period from c. 700 to c. 1000 C.E.

Both have lived in the Holy Land for centuries, the Jews for approximately three thousand years and the Arabs for about twelve hundred. The current hostility between them indicates that the present goal of each is not coexistence but retrieval of historic memories. The consequence has been violence, death, and suffering.

Yet the folktales of the two peoples can be housed in the same binding without guns and mortar shells. In my imagination, the metaphor inherent in this book will extend from the stories to the people whose creativity produced them.

*Coexistence as a Requisite of Survival*

It has become abundantly clear that in order to survive we must learn to live with others, frequently others who are different from ourselves. We have no choice, since there is no survival without coexistence.

On the level of family, a husband and a wife must learn the art of coexistence if their marriage is to survive. The circle broadens to include children and grandchildren, teachers, neighbors, classmates, teammates. All the thought and effort invested in "getting along" with friends, relatives, colleagues, and coworkers make coexistence the activity in which we expend much of our psychic energy.

On a global level, there are many examples of the failure to coexist peaceably: the Catholics and Protestants in Northern Ireland, the Moslems, Croats, and Serbs in Bosnia, the Iraqis and the Kurds, the Moslems and Christians in Lebanon, the blacks and whites in South Africa and indeed in the United States, the Armenians and the Turks, to mention just a few. The death and despair displayed on TV nightly are a grizzly testament to the desirability of coexistence. There is no viable alternative.

## HOW THIS BOOK EVOLVED:
## SOME PERSONAL EXPERIENCES

I must digress to a bit of autobiography. How did I come to feel so strongly that Jews and Arabs can and must learn the art of coexistence in order for both to survive and enjoy a desirable quality of life, enriched by each other's presence?

This attitude is undoubtedly part of a basic moral concept formed in childhood. In addition, the events of the summer of 1931 loom in my mind as powerful contributors to my development. They remain etched in my memory as if in stone. Let me try to transport you back with me.

## My First Contact with the Jews
## of Palestine and an Arab

Still in my teens, I am in Igls-bei-Innsbruck, Austria, an ocean and a half-continent away from New York where I have spent my life. I am here as companion to my sister, Rose Halprin, the newly elected national president of Hadassah. She is not well and her doctor has forbidden her attendance at the possibly overstimulating Zionist Congress being held in Basel.

We have traveled to a quiet inn in Igls where after the Congress disbands, Hadassah delegates from the United States and from Palestine will join Rose Halprin and Rose Jacobs, the outgoing president, to discuss future policy. Hitler is on the rise although not yet in power, and profound problems face the Jews of the world.

Since I am not involved with the Hadassah discussions, I take walks alone in the woods. There I see carved into the bark of tree after tree the German words *Tod zum Jude*—"Death to the Jew." I am enraged at the blatant boldness of the anti-Semitism, but somehow view it simply as a reminder of the Jewish experience of the past two thousand years, not as an augur of the unthinkable imminent decimation of European Jewry.

On one of my walks I am joined by Dr. Haim Yassky, the medical director of the Hadassah Hospital in Jerusalem. He invites me to visit his country and graciously offers to be my chaperone on the journey. I cable my father for permission: "Wonderful opportunity go Palestine great chaperone."

His response is a decisive "No!" I remember with gratitude my sister's reaction: she encourages me to go and promises to convince my father upon her return to the States that it was a good thing to do.

I embark on the most exciting and formative experience of my life.

Since I have very little money, I travel steerage on an Italian liner that plies the Mediterranean from Trieste to Jaffa. The sordidness of the cabin does not diminish my excitement or my happiness.

We never go below deck, anyway; we dance and sing way into the night until, exhausted, we fall asleep on deck chairs under the vivid Mediterranean sky. We are all very young and enthusiastic. I appear to be the only American on board who will be experiencing the Holy Land for the first time.

My chaperone, Dr. Yassky, invites me from time to time to have a meal with him in the first-class dining room. I meet many Jews returning from the Zionist Congress to their homes in Palestine: journalists, delegates representing the different parties, people from all walks of life.

On one of these occasions, I make the acquaintance of a Christian Arab, a Palestinian who is returning home to Jerusalem after four years at Oxford, where he has been studying the archaeology of the Near East. Contrary to my stereotypical concept, the first Arab I meet is not wearing a picturesque fez, *kaffiyeh*, or aba, not even a black mustache. Auburn-haired and clean-shaven, he is dressed in informal western clothes like everybody else on board. He is returning to take a job with the Antiquities Department of the British Mandate of Palestine.

We have a number of mutual interests. A student at Barnard College, I also attend classes at the nearby Jewish Theological Seminary. I too have been studying Bible and the history of the Near East. We converse on deck, leaning against the railing and looking out to sea.

One afternoon after lunch in first-class, Moshe Chertok, a journalist on the staff of *Davar*, the popular labor daily, invites me to be a fourth hand in an ongoing bridge game. I am not an experienced player and agree to help out on condition that the others conspire to let me fill the role of dummy, for which, I quip, I am well suited in the game.

As I approach the game table, a tall, thin man rises from his seat to his full height and says in a loud voice, "I refuse to play with a girl who talks with an Arab!" And he stalks away. I learn later that he is a prominent Jewish Palestinian agronomist.

Moshe Chertok casually helps me into one of the empty chairs, takes another for himself, and murmurs, "That's just fine. Now we have the opportunity of inviting as our fourth hand a person of character."

Some twenty to thirty years later our paths cross again in New York. By now Chertok has taken a Hebrew name, Moshe Sharett, and he is the foreign minister of Israel.

Curious, I venture to ask with some hesitation, "Mr. Sharett, do you remember me? Do I look at all familiar to you?"

His response is immediate. "Of course. You are the American girl on the boat! How could I forget the American girl on the boat?"

I am certain that there are more Sharetts among the Israelis than people like the agronomist.

### Kibbutz Mizra

The section of this book entitled "Arab Tales" probably germinated in my head in 1931–1932 during my first stay in Palestine, when I lived in Kibbutz Mizra. Our closest neighbors, in addition to Kibbutz Genigar, Tel Adashim, and other Jewish settlements in the Emek (the valley of Esdraelon), were Arabs who lived in a nearby village. I got to know them because we invited them to our celebrations and they returned the courtesy and the conviviality. At these parties, they told stories that revealed their ethnic creativity, and we told stories that revealed ours.

Together with some of my *chaverim*, members of my *kibbutz*, I went up regularly to the weekly Arab public market in Nazareth. There we traded horses and produce with the Arabs who lived in and around that small ancient town situated a mountain-climb above us. We exchanged stories as well.

In those years under the British mandate, there were three official languages: English, Arabic, and Hebrew. Since the residents educated under the mandate understood all three, language was not a barrier to our communication or to our storytelling. Between *debkas* and *horahs*, the two popular folk dances of the Arabs and the Jews, we heard tales from both groups.

We lamented bitterly the victims of the "riots" of 1929 and other sporadic terrorist acts by Arab extremists. Yet in most rural areas of the country and in urban communities, Arabs and Jews coexisted with considerable tolerance and mutual help. How else would the *yishuv* have been able to flourish as it did, or the Arabs to have experienced their heightened level of health and prosperity?

## Szold and Magnes

The key to my understanding the necessity for coexistence lies largely in the influence of two great Jews who made early *aliyah* to the Jewish *yishuv* in Palestine: Henrietta Szold, the founder and first president of Hadassah, the Women's Zionist Organization of America, and Yehudah Magnes, the first president of the Hebrew University in Jerusalem.

Both of these thoughtful leaders realized that as the *yishuv* grew, prospered, and presumably approached statehood, a legal plan for official coexistence would have to be formulated. The kind of country they envisaged for the Jews was one in which minorities would enjoy equality and respect; Jews would expect the same treatment from the Arab majorities in other countries in the Near East and North Africa.

Szold and Magnes accepted the inevitable presence of the Arabs in Palestine. They saw, hanging over the fragile Jewish settlement, a sword of Damocles that would surely fall should coexistence founder in the absence of mutual respect and support.

With the Magnes family I shared a friendship that permitted me to play tennis with their son on a private court. That opportunity alone was a privilege. In addition, during those visits, I heard the father's enthusiastic and instructive formulations about coexistence.

With Henrietta Szold I enjoyed a close relationship for the year and some months that I remained in the country. While I lived in Kibbutz Mizra, my meetings with her were sporadic. I had strict instructions that whenever I did get to Jerusalem I was to come directly to her suite in the Eden Hotel.

My trips from the Emek were usually made on Tenuva Cooperative milk delivery trucks, which arrived in Jerusalem at the wee hours of the morning. Although I hesitated to wake her so early, I nevertheless complied with Szold's wishes. I found her either working at her desk or giving her hair a hundred brush strokes, a daily custom. We would then get involved in a warm interaction, largely about life in the *kibbutz*, which she longed to experience firsthand but had never found the time.

Szold also expressed her ideas concerning the future of the Yishuv and her hope that the growing Jewish population would live in friendship and peace with the Arabs. She foresaw some of the current problems in the troubled land unless a plan for friendly coexistence were formulated and put into effect.

I am sure that Szold would have been gladdened by the establishment of the State of Israel and its many accomplishments since 1948. However, she would have been greatly saddened by the hostility and fighting that have scarred the land and its people. She would have wondered what happened to the ideas she and others grappled with so intensely as they sought a viable solution that would preempt violence and death.

As for me, at a young age I developed a firm belief that

some formula for coexistence was necessary in order to avoid bloodshed in the land of the Bible. Hopefully, peace would be the ultimate reward.

## Wars and Their Aftermath

Following two visits to Palestine in the thirties, I did not return to the land until the early 1950s, after World War II. It was also after the United Nations' November 1947 decision providing for partition into an Arab and a Jewish sector of what remained of Palestine. By far the largest sector, east of the Jordan River, called Transjordan, had already been partitioned off in 1920 and its name changed in 1946 to the Hashemite Kingdom of Jordan.

*The 1948 War.* Still another war had been fought, the 1948 war between the surrounding Arab countries and the very young Israel. Jordan, Syria, Egypt, Iraq, and Lebanon, opposed to the UN partition decision, had invaded the infant state of Israel the day it was proclaimed, May 14, 1948, the date of Britain's departure from Palestine.

After the ensuing battles and the victory of Israel on most fronts, several armistices had been signed in 1949, establishing legally recognized boundaries. A part of the disputed area was included in the State of Israel. The Gaza Strip was put under Egyptian administration. The West Bank and the eastern sector of Jerusalem, including the ancient walled city, were annexed by Jordan following its victory in the bloody, hard-fought battle for the Jewish quarter.

Hostility between Arabs and Jews had clearly exploded. My earlier notion of friendship and cooperation between them seemed unrealistic, perhaps unattainable.

*The 1967 War.* Enmity between Israel and its Arab neighbors escalated again in 1967, when Egypt closed off access to the Gulf of Aqaba, Israel's southern outlet to the Indian Ocean. As a result of the "Six-Day War" which ensued, the Israelis won the Gaza Strip and the West Bank. They also gained the ancient walled Jerusalem and the contiguous areas surrounding it, thus reuniting that divided city. The Golan Heights fell to them in the battle against Syria.

Together with other professors in the Boston-Cambridge area interested in peace in the Near East, I visited Israel within a few weeks after the fighting and experienced the aftermath of the war. Despite their exhilaration over the victories, many people, including Prime Minister David Ben Gurion, expressed concern about the pitfalls created by the conquest and about the future of coexistence.

*The Yom Kippur War.* In October 1973, on Yom Kippur, Egypt under Nasser attacked Israel in the south as Syria under Assad attacked from the north. After a few days of Arab advances, the tide turned and Israel achieved victory on both fronts. Through the intervention of the United States and the Soviet Union, the successful Israeli campaign was stopped and armistices were signed.

I had been visiting Israel since 1967, teaching summer courses in Tivon at Oranim, the *kibbutz* training school for psychologists and special education teachers. Although Israel emerged victorious in 1973, the atmosphere was saturated with gloom when I arrived there after the Yom Kippur War. The country was traumatized by its lack of readiness for the surprise attack.

No land was exchanged in the 1973 war; however, antagonisms were sharpened, and Israel's sense of insecurity heightened. It was apparent to me as a visitor that mutual hostility and distrust had increased.

*The War in the Persian Gulf.* During the Gulf War of 1991, the international spotlight focused on the Near East. It did not take long for the world's attention to shift to the Arab-Jewish conflict from its original concentration on Iraq's invasion of Kuwait and Saddam Hussein's survival despite his crushing military defeat. As interest in Hussein's perfidy waned, the world's attention centered on a series of meetings between Israel and the Arab countries concerning problems specific to each country and to the major regional problem of coexistence and peace.

*After the Wars.* There is widespread belief in Israel, as well as in the Diaspora, that there is no way of ruling another people against their will without distorting the spirit of Israel's founding fathers. The conviction persists, despite extremists on both sides, that Arabs and Jews can live side by side in the land, enriched by each other's presence.

Indeed, Arabs and Jews do coexist within the green line. They live peaceably in adjoining neighborhoods, sometimes next door to each other, in cities such as Jerusalem, Haifa, Jaffa, and Acre. They live peaceably in the countryside, where Arabic villages and Jewish settlements have coexisted since the first modern *aliyah* in the nineteenth century, and before that since biblical times.

Coexistence clearly seems a desirable alternative to the increasing hostility that escalated into the *intifada* in the territories and into reciprocal aggressive and deadly acts within the green line, even in Jerusalem, the city of peace.

The conviction that the only solution to the dilemma is for the two peoples to live side by side in peace has inspired me to work over the years with groups dedicated to this purpose: Givat Haviva, Neve Shalom/Wahat al Salaam, Interns for Peace, and the Jerusalem Foundation. Other organized efforts to accomplish the same end are achieving regional success in enclaves all over the land. The Abraham Fund, based in New York, has published a comprehensive directory of several hundred organizations engaged in activities that promote the peaceful coexistence of Arabs and Jews.

As this is written, Monday, September 13, 1993, has become a historic day in the process because of the handshake of Yasir Arafat, P.L.O. chairman, and Yitzhak Rabin, prime minister of Israel. I quote Thomas L. Friedman of the *New York Times*: "With one gesture it [the handshake] transformed the problem from an ideological struggle over who is the rightful owner of historic Palestine into a practical one over how to share the same living space."

## HISTORY

*Golden Years of Coexistence*
*under Mohammedanism*

History has a great deal to teach us about the possibility of coexistence.

Max I. Dimont wrote in his remarkable *Jews, God, and History* about the "improbable but true tale of a camel driver's establishment of a world empire in the name of Allah, wherein the Jews rose to their golden age of creativity, only to be plunged into a Dark Age with the eclipse of the Crescent and the ascent of the Cross."

From c. 700 to c. 1000 C.E. the Mohammedan faith spread from the Arabian peninsula across North Africa to Spain. The Jews enjoyed religious freedom and occupied posts of great eminence in the Moslem empire. Among those who rose to prominence during this period of coexistence was Maimonides (1135–1204), the great Jewish scholar, scientist, and philosopher, who served as physician to the king of Egypt.

*Dispersion*

By c. 1000 C.E., with the rise of aggressive Christianity, the Crusades to capture the Holy Land had been launched against both Moslem and Jewish "infidels." The Golden Age of Mohammedanism came to an end and with it the productive coexistence of Jews and Moslems, cosufferers during the onslaught of the Crusades.

The Crusades were followed by the Spanish Inquisition. Jews were tortured and given the choice of abandoning their religion by becoming Christians or being exiled and dispersed throughout the world. Approximately one-third remained in Spain and in Portugal as Marranos, or underground Jews.

Most of the Jews of both countries chose Diaspora and adherence to their ancient religion. They retained their longing to return to their biblical home, of which Jerusalem or Zion had been the symbol since the original dispersion from Judea by the Romans in 70 C.E.

## Return to the Land

During the last part of the nineteenth century, their longing took concrete political form in a movement to settle in their ancient land. The atrocities in Europe during the twentieth century accelerated the process. Remnants of Jewish communities from all parts of Europe streamed into Palestine and grasped the welcoming hands held out to them by the *yishuv*. Sephardic Jews from Africa, Asia, and the Near East joined the ingathering, adding to its heterogeneity.

The recent Russian and Ethiopian immigrations to Israel increased the population and its complexity. The need for coexistence and mutual help ballooned not only for Jews and Arabs, but for Jews coming from different countries, backgrounds, and experiences. Many of them had lived side by side with Arabs for centuries and had to adjust to life with European Jews whom they met for the first time in Israel.

## MORE AUTOBIOGRAPHY: THE JEWISH STORIES

I believe I originally started the Jewish tales in this book when I was ten years old. It was then that I heard the first eleven stories and became excited about them. These tales buzzed around in my head for many years, seeking release in writing.

Finally, during my three-year stint as a visiting lecturer at Harvard, I took a summer off and wrote them in my own fashion. They turned out to be quite different from the original versions. My retelling of these stories was published in a small volume in 1970 by Little, Brown and Co.

Those stories are included in the present collection as illustrative of the literary tradition of Jewish folklore. Even after folktales have been written down in one language, they are subject to retelling and reinterpretation in the same and other languages by storytellers of future generations. One need not be a professional folklorist to tell a good story as it bubbles up.

Dov Noy, the Grunwald Professor of Folklore at the Hebrew University, analyzed my version of "The Witches of Ascalon," the first story in the next section. If you are interested in the way folktales change from storyteller to storyteller, see the analysis in his foreword on page 6.

The second group of Jewish stories, subsumed under the title "Folk Festival in Sedot Mikhah," were collected in Israel after World War II. These eleven stories were selected from thousands related orally by Jews who streamed into the country from Europe and by Jews who were flown in from Moslem countries.

The immigration from Russia, the Ukraine, Poland, Hungary, Germany, the Netherlands, etc., and from Iraq, Turkey, Kurdistan, Libya, Ethiopia, etc., brought not only people to Israel, but their folklore as well. The new settlers told their stories to collectors for the Israel Folktale Archives, as well as at festivals held periodically at Sedot Mikhah in the Judean hills. One of these cultural celebrations is imagined in this section of the book.

## ONE LAST WORD

I disclaim any pretension at being a professional folklorist. I am a psychologist and professor of psychology who appreciates good stories and likes to weave them into her own tapestry.

Both Arab and Jewish stories are, in my opinion, among the best in the world, the richest, the most colorful, sometimes sad, sometimes funny, but always essentially human. I enjoy telling them in my own fashion as storytellers and troubadours have always done. How else can we account for the numerous extant versions of "Cinderella"?

I hope that, after reading this book, you, too, become a storyteller. You can then relate these very tales in your own idiosyncratic style to children or to any interested audience.

For the moment, enjoy reading them. Savor the differences and similarities in the plots, backgrounds, social customs, humor, and beliefs of two peoples, whose histories have brought them in close proximity for thousands of years.

The Bible tells of Abraham, from whom both are descended. It tells of his wives, Sarah and Hagar, and their sons, Isaac and Ishmael, who started the separation into two nations, one on the east and one on the west bank of the Jordan. We learn in Genesis 25:9 that his sons Isaac and Ishmael came together after many years of separation and "buried him in the cave of Machpelah." The Bible also tells of the two sons of Isaac, Jacob and Esau, who quarreled and later became reconciled.

In the Bible, too, we learn the story of Naomi the Israelite and Ruth, her Moabite daughter-in-law, who said the unforgettable words, "Whither thou goest I will go." The widow Ruth married another Israelite, Boaz, and one of their descendants was the quintessentially human King David of Israel. Another was Jesus of Nazareth, who started a related set of beliefs and a new religion.

There must be some symbolic meaning to all this interrelatedness. There is much to think of and even more to do.

# I

# JEWISH TALES

# Old Tales from the Middle East and Later Tales from Europe

# FOREWORD

It is a privilege to participate in the writing of this landmark book. I use the word "landmark," because for the first time Arab and Jewish tales can be read side by side in a single attractive volume. Furthermore, they are narrated by a writer who has known the Near East for many years and has been sensitive to the cultures of both peoples. She has a vision that they can and must coexist peacefully in the present and the future, as they have in the past.

Blanche Serwer-Bernstein showed her appreciation of stories handed down in her own culture in her first volume, *Let's Steal the Moon*, published in 1970 by Little, Brown. I am delighted that they are being reintroduced to the general reading public now in the first section of the current volume.

In my introduction to a 1989 paperback reprinting of *Let's Steal the Moon*, I wrote enthusiastically about this remarkable collection of eleven Jewish tales. Now, in 1993, I read them with the same pleasure and excitement that I experienced when I first came upon them twenty-three years ago, shortly after their original publication. It was a pioneering accomplishment bringing a remarkable sample of Jewish folk literature to the attention of the American reading public.

Dr. Serwer-Bernstein wrote the stories, intertwining them masterfully with her own literary-esthetic values and psychological insights. And no wonder! She is a clinical psychologist whose rich academic career includes teaching a course in children's literature at Harvard.

The selection of these eleven tales is culled from many countries and centuries. It includes ancient legends about King Solomon (First Temple), Rabbi Simon Ben Shetah, and Hillel the Elder (Second Temple), as well as relatively recent anecdotes from Eastern Europe. The narratives take the reader to Jerusalem and Ascalon in the Holy Land, to Prague in Czechoslovakia, to Chelm in Poland, and to a *shtetl* in Russia.

Among the acting characters we have supernatural beings like Ashmodai, the demon king. There are also historical heroes like Napoleon, whose life is saved by a Jewish tailor during the 1812 Russian campaign.

In addition to its range of time, place, and cultural heritage, the great charm of these stories lies in the author's style of adaptation. Comparing the opening tale, "The Witches of Ascalon," with its original midrashic version, we notice the added rhymed dialogue between the Rabbi and the witches, the magic formulas used in the confrontation between men and demons, and other effects unique to Dr. Serwer-Bernstein's tale. Her innovative techniques are stylistic characteristics of orally transmitted folk tales, and she uses them masterfully.

Changes occur in the contents, too. The midrashic plot ends with the annihilation of the eighty witches by the young disciples of the Rabbi, and the word "killing" figures explicitly in the original text. Not so in the elegant retelling in this version: "Then the young men, whirling wildly with their witches, lifted them high and carried them through the storm to the top of a mountain, high up against the sky. . . ."

The end of the story reflects, as folktale endings generally do, the wishful thinking and the ethnosocial ideals of the reading or listening audience: "Ascalon was rid of the eighty witches." The world was no longer afraid of their power of mischief. The witches continue, however, to live somewhere as harmless beings, where they "make designs against the moon."

The stories in this exciting collection were originally told as part of the literary and cultural heritage that the author passed on to her three sons, as she states in her foreword. The same is true now, as she retells them to her five grandchildren. They enjoy listening as their parents and the general reader did one generation ago. Each generation is a link in the golden chain of Jewish tradition. Because the folk-literary sources are elegantly presented, these stories make our linking to the chain all the more enjoyable.

Dov Noy

# DEAR READERS

You may be wondering how I know these old, old stories. As a very little girl, I heard some of them from my family. I was the youngest of eight children and was often treated to a story by a parent, brother, or sister.

There were many well-worn books in my home. When I was old enough, I read them and recognized some of the tales that had been told to me.

Many years later, I had three boys of my own, Philip, the oldest, Daniel, the middle son, and Jeremy, the youngest. They liked the stories very much, too.

The mechanical man, for example. He was more real to us than was his master, the Maharal. We imagined the Golem becoming more and more human, until he loved children as if he were a real man. How unhappy we were when he was put to rest in the attic of the Prague synagogue! When I was in Prague some years later, I thought of climbing up to look under the old prayer book pages for the huge clay figure. Then I remembered that the Maharal had forbidden it.

"The Witches of Ascalon" had always been told to me in just a few words. But I pictured the eighty witches shrieking out their challenges gleefully until they were carried off by Simon's young men. I wrote the story as I had imagined it.

And so with the rest of the tales.

It would be hard, really impossible, for me to tell you

exactly who created the stories. They came down to us because they were told by parents to children and by teachers to pupils. Then someone wrote them down for others to read and tell again, each in his or her own fashion.

# Tales about Witches
# and Demons

# 1

# THE WITCHES
# OF ASCALON

Can you imagine what it would be like if eighty witches lived nearby and flew about every night, making witch designs against the moon?

Long ago, this is exactly what happened to the people of Ascalon, a city in ancient Israel. The witches inhabited a cave just outside the city and plagued the people with mischief, putting salt in their dessert, sugar in their meat, and wine in their animal fodder.

Rabbi Simon decided to rid Ascalon of this plague of witches. Finally he had an idea. It was a simple plan, but it required a heavy downpour of rain. He waited for the wet season.

On a very stormy day he called together eighty handsome young men. To each one he gave a clean white robe folded inside a clay urn. Together they went to the witches' cave on the outskirts of Ascalon. Each youth carried the clay vessel upside down on his head, so that both he and his robe would remain dry.

Rabbi Simon said to the eighty young men, "You wait out here. I will enter the cave alone. When you hear me whistle once, put on your clean dry robes. When you hear my second whistle, rush into the cave. Each of you seize a witch and dance with her. Lift her high up in the air as you whirl, for a witch can do no harm if she is held above the ground."

At the entrance to the cave, Rabbi Simon called out to the witches, "Open, open, for a friendly wizard!"

The witches peered out and chanted,

"Witches' brew, snakes and frogs;
Who is that in all-dry togs?"

The Rabbi sang aloud,

"Wizard's answer straight and true:
Let me share your tasty brew."

The witches let out a long, raucous laugh and chanted,

"Witches' brew, sorrow and pain;
Who stays dry in storm and rain?"

Simon incanted, grinning a demon's grin,

"Wizard's answer straight and true:
Wizard dries up rain and dew."

The witches then shrieked in earsplitting tones,

"Witches' brew, warts and hair;
Why are you standing there?"

Calmly, Simon's voice rang out,

"Wizard's answer straight and true:
I am here to learn from you."

Satisfied, the witches invited him in and all eighty of them danced wildly around him in a circle, chanting,

"Wizard defies stormy weather;
Witches, wizard drink together.

Wizard walks 'tween drops of rain;
Witches wish his power to gain."

Convinced that he had walked between the drops of rain, the witches agreed to teach him their witchcraft if he would teach them his wizardry. Each prepared to show her most cherished skill.
One witch chanted,

"Water and wheat together knead!
Ten loaves of bread, witches feed!"

On the table there suddenly appeared ten loaves of bread, steaming hot.
Another witch chanted,

"Beef, lamb or veal: the meat
You want is here to eat!"

Platters of delicious roast beef, lamb and veal in thick gravies joined the bread on the gleaming white cloth.
A third witch chanted,

"Fruits: banana, orange, date and fig,
Easy for me, like dancing a jig!"

Now beautiful bowls of luscious fruit made the table bright with color.
A fourth witch chanted,

"Will you with the witches dine?
We will need some jugs of wine."

Sweet-smelling wine in huge clay jugs stood tempting them in the cool darkness of the cave.
Then all the witches chanted together,

"Snails and moles are wizards' brew;
Now show us what *you* can do."

Rabbi Simon chanted,

"Merrymaking is what you need;
Eighty young men for you are freed!
Wondrous marvel is this deed!
They come dry through raindrops, heed!"

He whistled once, and the boys put on their white robes.
He whistled a second time, and they all rushed into the cave.
Simon sang out in merry tones,

"Round and round he takes in dance
Each his witch up high to prance.
Swing her high, take no chance
Above the ground she's in a trance."

Then the young men, whirling wildly with their witches,
lifted them high and carried them through the storm to the
top of a mountain, high up against the sky. There they could
make designs against the moon but they no longer had the
power of mischief.

This is how Ascalon was rid of the eighty witches.

# 2

# THE KING OF
# THE DEMONS AND
# THE WORM SHAMIR

Shamir was a worm so tiny that when asleep it looked like a grain of barley. Yet this small creature had the magical power to split the hardest rock.

Shamir was called upon to carve the Ten Commandments on two huge slabs of granite, because metal tools, symbols of war and death, could not be used. Then the little worm disappeared.

Two hundred and fifty years passed.

King Solomon was planning to build a Temple of Peace in Jerusalem. He must cut down great rocks in the mountains and huge trees in the forest. Only Shamir could help him split marble and wood without metal tools.

Although famed for his wisdom and knowledge, Solomon did not know the whereabouts of the wonderful wee worm. He called his advisers to him.

One wise old man counseled, "We cannot help you, King Solomon. No man knows where Shamir is. Only the Demons know the secrets of the heavens above, of the earth below, and of the waters under the earth. Call upon them to help you."

The King knew how to summon the Demons. He turned the dazzling signet ring which he wore on his finger three times in one direction and three times in the other.

A mighty wind swirled about him and the earth below him rumbled and shook. Then before him stood two genii.

"What is your will, O King?" they asked.

"Tell me where I can find the worm Shamir."

The genii trembled. "We cannot help you, King Solomon. Only our ruler, Ashmodai, knows where Shamir is."

"Where does Ashmodai, King of the Demons, live?" asked Solomon.

"Far far away, on the top of a high, craggy mountain," replied the genii. "There our King Ashmodai has dug a deep well. Every evening, he drinks the pure water and then seals the mouth of the well with a huge rock. During the day, he flies to the ends of the earth, beyond the Great Sea, and even ascends to heaven. When the sun goes down in the western sky, he returns. He carefully examines the rock which seals the well to make sure that no one has touched it. Then he drinks the pure water. In the morning, he leaves on his journeys again."

In a rush of wind and with a thundering quake of the earth, the two genii disappeared.

Solomon summoned Benaiah, his trusted friend. He told of Ashmodai, King of the Demons, who lived on the lofty mountain and drank clear water from a sealed well.

"Go, Benaiah, and bring back the Demon King Ashmodai, for only he can tell us the whereabouts of Shamir. Take with you this bundle of wool, these skins of wine, and this golden chain, as well as my signet ring. You will need them on this quest."

Benaiah, friend of Solomon, traveled across the still desert for days, making his way over burning sand and dry brush. Then he reached a deep, dark forest. Finally he came to the Demon King's steep mountain. He climbed for days on the wooded slope. At the summit beyond the timberline, he found Ashmodai's well. How could he get into it without moving the rock which sealed the opening?

First, he dug, on the lower slope of the mountain, a pit leading upward to the floor of the well. He drained off the water and plugged the hole with wool. Then, higher up, he dug another pit, leading down to the Demon's emptied well. Into it he poured the wine from the skins he carried with him. Then Benaiah hid behind a large crag and waited for the King of the Demons.

As the shadows of evening began to fall, the Demon King Ashmodai flew down through the light of the stars and the moon. Finding the sealed well untouched, he rolled back the rock and went down to drink. Overcome by thirst, he gulped large amounts of the sweet, intoxicating liquor. He soon fell into a deep sleep.

Benaiah came from his hiding place and fastened the golden chain around Ashmodai's neck as he slept, sealing it with Solomon's golden signet ring.

When the Demon King awoke, he could not get up. Realizing that he was under a spell, he writhed in anger. His fierce struggle shook the mountains for miles around. The genii of the sea and air flew into the mountain caverns, where they cowered in fear for their King Ashmodai.

"Your struggles are useless, mighty King of the Demons," said Benaiah. "You must come with me to King Solomon."

Ashmodai breathed a deep sigh that scattered the leaves and the birds in all directions. Finally he said, "I am calm now and shall go with you. But I warn you that no good can come of this. Demons are not meant to walk on earth like human beings."

Together they traveled toward the holy city of Jerusalem, Benaiah, Solomon's friend, and Ashmodai, King of the Demons.

Wherever they went Ashmodai left a trace of destruction. If he touched a flower, it withered and died. When he leaned against a tree, he uprooted it.

In a town marketplace, they passed a happy wedding party. Ashmodai burst into tears.

"Why do you cry?" asked Benaiah.

"In three days the bridegroom will die because of me," answered Ashmodai.

In the next town, they overheard a man giving a shoe-maker an order for a pair of shoes that would last seven years. Ashmodai smiled bitterly.

"That man asks for shoes to last seven years. How should he know that he will die within a week because of my passing?"

Saddened by his effect on mankind, Ashmodai tried to be kind. He helped a blind man who was bewildered and lost. He guided a drunkard through the heavy traffic at a crossroad. Once he passed a group of bullies teasing a small child. He stopped to give the little boy to his mother.

On this long journey, Benaiah began to like and respect Ashmodai, King of the Demons.

Benaiah and Ashmodai finally arrived at King Solomon's palace. The King of the Demons stood face-to-face with the King of Israel and reproached him, saying, "Mighty King, are you not satisfied with ruling man? Must you rule the Spirits and Demons as well?"

"Do not be angry," said Solomon. "I need your help. I plan to build a Temple of Peace, and therefore cannot use metal tools, symbols of war, to hew the marble and wood. I need the wonderful worm Shamir."

"But I do not have Shamir," protested Ashmodai.

"Tell me where the tiny creature is hidden, and you will be freed," persuaded Solomon.

Ashmodai said reluctantly, "Shamir has belonged to the Prince of the Sea ever since it carved the Ten Command-ments on two tablets of stone. High on a solitary mountain-top, the Prince's woodcock, a faithful bird, guards the little creature closely. He keeps it under his wing, so that it will be safe as he flies about."

"Where is this mountain summit on which the wood-cock guards Shamir for the Prince of the Sea?" asked Solomon.

"Far beyond the haunts of man, where only Demons find their way," replied Ashmodai.

"Then you yourself must go and get Shamir, for the

Temple of Peace cannot be built without it," urged Solomon. "I will not release you until you bring the magical worm to me."

Ashmodai, longing to be free again, said, "You force me to do this for you, King Solomon. Prepare for me, then, a hard glass cover the size of a bird's nest, some wood, and a small box made of lead."

The earth shook and the winds raged as Ashmodai whirled into the air and flew across forest wastes and pathless seas. At last, on the summit of a mountain so high that the stars were reflected in its smooth rocks, he found the woodcock's nest; in it, alone, seven tiny fledglings chirped for their food.

Ashmodai covered the nest with the piece of glass so that when the bird returned he would be able to see his babies but not to feed them. The Demon King then hid behind a rock.

Soon the woodcock flew back to his nest. He saw his helpless young but could not get to them through the strong glass. He screeched loudly, flapping his wings wildly. The baby birds, hungry and frightened by the noise, chirped pitifully.

The woodcock tried to break the glass by hammering at it with his beak and smashing his body against it. Ashmodai watched him while he beat at it, hour after hour, until there was no breath left in him. The fledglings quieted down, weak with hunger and fear.

The woodcock knew his babies would die if he did not feed them soon. He must get into the nest immediately. Reluctantly, he took the precious Shamir from under his wing and placed it on the hard glass. He watched carefully as the glass was split into a thousand pieces. He poised to catch the wonderful worm, entrusted to his care by the Prince of the Sea.

At that moment, Ashmodai uttered a frightening cry. Startled, the woodcock dropped Shamir. Ashmodai caught the worm as it fell, wrapped it in wool, and placed it in the box of lead.

Then he rose into the air. The woodcock flew after him in a brave but vain effort to get Shamir back.

Whirling over hill and plain, Ashmodai finally arrived in Jerusalem and delivered the magical worm to Solomon. With its help, the King built the Temple. Ashmodai remained with King Solomon until the Temple was completed, hoping to return Shamir to the woodcock who had guarded it so carefully for the Prince of the Sea.

However, after its work was done, the tiny worm disappeared. To this day, no one knows where it is to be found. Perhaps someday it will be used again to split the rock for a monument to peace.

# Tales about
# Changes in Men

# 3

# THE MERCHANT WITH NOTHING TO SELL

Many years ago, a ship on the high seas carried merchants to foreign parts and with them their merchandise to sell abroad. All day long, the merchants stood talking in groups on the vessel's deck. They boasted of their silks, their precious gems, their silver and gold dishes, and other riches which were stored in the ship's hold.

Sometimes the ocean was calm without a ripple of movement. At other times it was stormy, and the waves rose high above the ship. Still they talked of their fortunes.

Among them was one passenger who listened, but did not speak. If asked about his work or his fortune, he would answer, "Like you, I am a merchant with valuable things to sell." But he carried no silks, no precious gems, no silver and gold dishes or other riches.

The merchants laughed aloud. "Where, then, is your merchandise?" they jeered. "How can you be a merchant when you have nothing to sell?"

Every day they mocked him. "A merchant with nothing to sell!" they teased.

He smiled and said, "My merchandise is more precious than yours, though it fills no space in the hold."

One day, a black-sailed vessel stopped the merchants' ship. Marauding pirates came aboard and robbed them of everything, all the silks, precious gems, gold and silver dishes and jewelry. Stripped of their personal possessions, the merchants were lucky to remain alive. Clad in rags, they could no longer boast of their riches.

Soon the ship landed in the foreign port where they were to have sold their possessions and amassed great fortunes. Instead, they filed down the gangplank in their torn, makeshift garb and walked to the city.

What were they to do? A kind man stopped and gave them a coin. Soon they became beggars, walking from house to house, getting food where they could. Sometimes they starved; sometimes they ate the berries in the fields outside the city. But always they talked of their past riches and splendor, lost to the pirates.

The merchant who had carried no goods with him also went into the city. But he did not beg. Since he was a well-educated man, his merchandise was stored in his mind. He walked directly to the House of Study, where he met other learned men. They were amazed at the extent of his knowledge and soon asked him to join them in teaching and studying. They gave him clothing, food, and lodging. Before many months had passed, he became a highly respected man in his new country. He walked in the streets with scholars and enjoyed the honors heaped upon him.

One day, he chanced to meet some of the merchants who had mocked him during the journey on board the merchant vessel. They expressed great surprise at his happy and prosperous appearance.

"How did you succeed so quickly in achieving fame and fortune in this new land?" they asked in amazement.

His answer was simply, "Did I not tell you that my merchandise was more valuable than yours?"

# 4

# THE WIND AND
# THE ANT

In the days when Solomon was King, he ruled over every creature in the world, over the sons of men and the beasts and the birds.

Solomon had a great mantle to sit upon, sixty miles long and sixty miles wide. It was of green silk, woven with fine gold and embroidered with beautiful figures.

When he traveled, his throne was on the mantle. Solomon sat on the throne surrounded by thousands of his men, and the mantle, bearing all of them, rode on the wind. They took the meal of the morning in Damascus far to the east, and the meal of the evening in Medea far to the west.

One day, as the wind bore him and his men aloft above the earth, Solomon boasted, "Behold, there is no one like me in the world, for I have wisdom and understanding and I rule over all creatures. Only I travel wind-borne above the lowly and see the earth stretching beneath me."

At that moment the wind withdrew from him, and forty thousand men fell off the mantle. When Solomon saw this, he cried out to the wind, "Return, O wind, and be quiet!"

The wind answered him, saying, "Solomon, stop your boasting; then I will return to you."

Solomon was shamed by the wind.

Another day as he was traveling, he passed over a valley swarming with ants. He heard the voice of a black ant

27

saying to her companions, "Enter into your houses or you will be crushed by the hosts of King Solomon."

Then Solomon was angry, and he said to the wind, "Descend to the earth," and the wind descended.

He sent after the ants and said to them, "Which of you was it that said to the others, 'Enter into your houses or the armies of Solomon will crush you'?"

The ant that had spoken answered, "It was I who said this to my companions."

He asked, "Why did you say that?"

She answered, "Because I felt that they would look at your great armies and fear you, forgetting that you are only a man, son of man."

He asked her, "Why amongst all the ants did you alone speak?"

She answered, "Because I am their queen."

He said to her, "What is your name?"

She answered, "Machshamah."

He said to her, "Queen Machshamah, I wish to ask you a question."

She said, "It is not fitting that the one who asks should be seated high on his throne, and the one who is asked should be below on the ground. Take me in your hand and I will answer you."

Then Solomon lifted her up and took her into his hand, so that she faced him, and she said, "Ask what you wish."

He said to her, "Is there in the world anyone greater than I?"

She said to him, "Yes."

He said, "Who is it?"

She answered, "It is I."

Then Solomon cried out in anger, "How are you, an ant, greater than I, King of Men?"

She replied, "If I were not greater than you are, you would not have lifted me up as you did."

When Solomon heard the words of the ant he was enraged, and threw her down, and said to her, "Ant, you do not know who I am; I am Solomon, son of David the King!"

She said to him, "Remember then that you were born from a common man and stop boasting."

Solomon fell on his face. He was shamed by the words of the ant.

Then the ant said to Solomon, "Go, but do not forget that you are a man, son of man, no more or less than other men."

Solomon commanded the wind, "Lift up the mantle and let us go."

But the wind would not lift up the mantle, for he said, "Solomon, you boast even to the tiny ant. No longer will you be borne aloft above your fellowmen. You must walk upon the earth like all men and feel your kinship with them. Then will you have the wisdom and understanding to rule over the creatures of the earth."

The air grew black and a roaring wind whirled Solomon spiraling upward and hurled him a thousand miles away. And Solomon became a beggar, unknown and uncared for, traveling in unknown lands.

"Good people, kind people," he would plead, "do not pass me by. I am Solomon, King of Israel."

People laughed. "You are king of the beggars," they mocked.

And Solomon, with memories of his great power, traveled alone, eating the berries of the field, roots, and nuts, drinking the pure waters of mountain streams, and cleansing himself in rivers and lakes.

In his wanderings, Solomon crossed a large expanse of desert. In the solitude of the wilderness, he sat down upon the sand. Nearby, he saw a hill of ants swarming busily in and out, carrying sand grains and ant eggs, in constant movement, helping each other in their work.

He thought to himself, "What am I here on earth? I am but as a speck of sand in the desert, as a blade of grass in the field. I am no greater than these busy ants who build for each other's happiness."

He felt a great warmth, a love for all things both big and

small in the world about him. He was lonely and longed for Jerusalem and its people.

Suddenly, he felt a strong gust of wind which swirled about him and called, "Solomon, follow me and I will guide you back to your people."

Solomon followed the wind which led him to the city of Jerusalem. Alone he walked through the streets and looked about with love and understanding.

Then did Solomon become a king who could sing to his people:

> "Come my beloved, let us go forth into the fields,
> Let us lodge in the village . . .
>
> Set me as a seal upon thine heart,
> As a seal upon thine arm.
> For love is as strong as death."

# 5

# ASK A FOOLISH QUESTION

Once there lived a great Jewish scholar-hero called Rav Hillel. He was not known for his boldness or courage, but rather for his patience and mildness. He never showed anger, because he felt that kindness, like the mild rays of the sun, warms and expands the hearts of men.

Hillel was loved and respected because of his goodness. But there were people who did not understand how he could always be so patient. Frequently somebody would try to make him lose his temper.

One day a man challenged him, "I want you to tell me the whole of Jewish learning while I stand on one leg. Then and only then will I respect your wisdom."

Instead of showing anger at this unreasonable request, Hillel remained calm. He thought for a while and then said, "Keep this commandment: 'Do not do to others what you would not like them to do to you.' That is all you need to know. Now go and follow this commandment, and you will be a great and learned man in Israel."

The man obeyed and became Hillel's devoted student.

Hillel was well known throughout the world. From far away Rome came a scholar who also decided to provoke Hillel to anger. He said, "I came here because of your great fame for wisdom. But I am disappointed. Why is it that you think as a Jew and not simply as a man?"

"What you are really asking," said the rabbi in a soft voice, "is why we Hebrews do not admire the Roman art and culture. May I answer you with a story?

"A long time ago, when the world was young, there was a concert at the edge of the woods. The performer was a beautiful bluebird. In the audience were all the animals of the forest. The lion was there and the camel, the fox and the crow—even the fish in the nearby brook raised their heads to listen.

"The bluebird gave a magnificent performance. It sang so beautifully that even the pigeons cried, and as you know, they have no tears.

"But way down in the darkness of a small bush, hidden under a big leaf, there was a little worm with a sad face. When the concert was over, all the creatures applauded by roaring or hissing, growling or squeaking. Not so the worm. It just stared.

"A nearby weed wearing a big red flower watched the worm for a while and then spoke out, 'You worms are certainly peculiar. How can you remain glum in the midst of this beautiful music? Everybody else seems to be enjoying it.'

"The worm turned and said to the weed, 'All of you can listen to the music and enjoy it, but I know that when he is finished the bluebird is going to *eat* me!'"

The Roman smiled. Never again did he try to provoke Hillel. He understood that the outwardly calm man was letting him know his inner fears. The two men became close friends.

Still another man was convinced that Hillel could be made to show anger instead of kindness. He decided to try arousing Hillel's temper. He bet four hundred *zuzim* that he would bring the scholar to express rage.

The next day he burst into Hillel's house without knocking. "Where is Hillel? Where is Hillel?" he called, leaving off the title of Rav or Rabbi in order to show disrespect.

It was Friday afternoon, and Hillel was dressing for the Sabbath. He seemed not to notice the stranger's rudeness. Putting on his shirt, he said in his usual kind manner, "My son, what is it you wish?"

"I want to know," the man shouted, "why the Babylonians have round heads."

"My son, you have asked a good question," commented Hillel calmly. "The Babylonians have very complicated thoughts. They think in circles. Therefore they have round heads."

The man saw that Hillel had his own way of being angry. When asked a foolish question, instead of losing his temper, he gave a foolish answer in return.

The intruder went away. In a few minutes, he burst in again, calling more shrilly than before, "Where is Hillel? Where is Hillel?"

The scholar put on his sandals and asked, "What do you want, my son?"

"I want to know," bellowed the man, "why the people of Tadmor have round eyes."

Hillel responded, "My son, again you have asked a good question. I will tell you. They live in a sandy country. If they had eyes with two corners like ours, they could not remove the sand the wind blows into their eyes, and they would become blind."

Once more, Hillel had shown his annoyance by his reply but nevertheless had remained calm.

The man went away disappointed.

After a little while he came back, hoping to anger Hillel by continual interruptions while he was dressing. He roared raucously, "Where is Hillel? I want Hillel!"

Hillel came out to meet him, putting on his long robe. "My son, what do you wish of me?"

"I want to know why the Phrygians have broad feet."

"You have asked another good question," Hillel replied graciously. "The Phrygians live in moors and swamps. They have broad soles on their feet so that they can walk about more easily. If they had narrow feet, they would sink into the marshes."

Once again the man understood that Hillel was letting his anger out in his own fashion. He could not help but admire Hillel's cool, unruffled temper.

Then he remembered the money he was about to lose and shouted furiously, "Are you the Hillel who calls himself Prince of the Israelites?"

"Yes," answered Hillel, still without raising his voice.

"Well, then," the man mocked. "I hope Israel will not produce any more people like you!"

"Why do you say that?" Hillel inquired good-humoredly.

"Because," blurted the stranger, "because through your kindness to me, I have lost four hundred *zuzim!*"

"Your money is not entirely lost," Hillel observed, smiling gently. "You will be wiser in the future and not make foolish wagers."

He got up and added in a low voice, "Don't you think it is better that you lose some money than that I lose my temper?"

Then Hillel put on his headdress and left for the Sabbath eve service.

# Tales Hard to Believe

# 6

# THE MECHANICAL MAN
# OF PRAGUE

The Maharal was a great Rabbi who lived in Prague about four hundred years ago. He loved his people and wanted to improve their lives because they were very poor and suffered great cruelty at the hands of their neighbors.

The Jews were attacked at Passover time each year, when the death of any Christian child was blamed on them. Many of them were tortured or killed by burning because of false accusations of child murder. One man was especially eager to bring undeserved punishment to the Jews. He was a meat slaughterer called John, whose wickedness brought them great fear and unhappiness.

One night the Maharal thought about this problem deep into the morning hours. At dawn, when he finally fell asleep, he heard in a dream the mystical words of the Cabala, a language of miracles, telling him to "create a Golem out of clay who will protect your people against their enemies." A Golem was a mechanical man who would obey his every wish.

Now most people would not have understood the language of the Cabala, since it was known only to the very scholarly. Not only did the Maharal understand, but he could recognize deep in these words a mystical formula by means of which he could create the Golem. For the making of a Golem all the four elements of Fire, Water, Air and Earth were necessary.

He therefore confided his secret to his son-in-law, Isaac ben Shimshon Ha-Cohen, who was born under the constellation of Fire, and to his disciple, Jacob ben Chaim Ha-Levi, who was born under the constellation of Water. The Maharal himself was born under the constellation of Air.

The three men, silent with the mystical secrets of the Cabala, went down to the River Moldau. There they molded with the clay of the riverbank a great figure of a man six feet long. They sculpted every part of his body in detail, the features of his face, his hands and feet.

Then all three stood at the feet of the prone Golem. The Maharal instructed Isaac to walk around the figure from right to left and as he circled to chant:

"Fire and water, fire and water,
Enter into this inert matter.
Give him life to help the Jews;
Into this Golem, life infuse!"

Immediately, the Golem began to glow like fire.

Then the Maharal ordered Jacob to encircle the figure from left to right, chanting another formula:

Water and fire, water and fire,
Soften this clod of hardened mire,
A creature to protect each child,
And guard against rumors wild."

A cloud of steam rose from the Golem's body.

Next, the Maharal himself circled the Golem seven times, and recited: "'And he breathed into his nostrils the breath of life; and man became a living soul.'"

The Golem opened his eyes and looked at the three men. The Maharal took from his cloak a parchment on which he had written a magical word. Inserting it into the forehead of the Golem, he commanded, "Get up on your feet!"

The Golem stood silent and motionless. They dressed him in clothes that were suitable for a custodian of the Synagogue.

Three had left Prague at dawn; at dusk four returned through the cold gray stone streets.

As they walked, the Maharal told the Golem solemnly, "We have created you so that you may protect the Jews against their enemies. We shall call you Joseph, and you will serve me in the Synagogue. You must obey me no matter what I tell you to do."

The Golem understood the words, although he could not speak. He soon became a familiar figure, sitting in a corner of the entrance hall to the Synagogue, mute and motionless, his head in his hands. The people called him Joseph the Speechless.

In the months that followed, the Maharal used the Golem secretly to protect the Jews of Prague. Sometimes he made him invisible by means of an amulet engraved with a mystical word from the Cabala, which the Golem wore around his neck.

The Maharal issued strict orders that the Golem must not be used for menial tasks. He must be ready at all times for an emergency.

The Rabbi's wife, Perele, disobeyed, however. One day, before Passover, when she was working very hard, she ordered the Golem to fetch water from the well to fill two big barrels in the pantry. What a help that would be to her in her housework!

Joseph the Golem snatched two buckets and ran to the well. Back and forth he trudged from the well to the barrels in the pantry. Perele was busy and nobody else took notice. Soon the barrels began to overflow and the water spread throughout the house.

Everybody shouted, "Stop, Joseph! Enough, Golem, enough!" But the Golem heeded no one until the Maharal, summoned by one of his students, ran in and stopped him with a mystical incantation.

Now they all breathed a sigh of relief that no one had been hurt. It became clear to them that danger lurked in their friend the Golem if he were used for any purpose other than the one for which he had been created.

As the Feast of Passover approached, the Maharal feared that some child in the city might die. The Jews would be blamed and their suffering would be great.

The Rabbi chanted mystical words of the Cabala into the ears of the Golem: "No harm must come to a child of Prague." The Golem understood.

The Maharal ordered Joseph to put on the clothes of an ordinary porter and to wander about the city, guarding every corner of it. Joseph roamed the streets at night, on the alert for any danger that might threaten the children of Prague. His hearing was sharp and he listened well. His nose was very sensitive and the smells of the city came to him from afar.

The week before Passover, the Golem was roaming through the poorest section of Prague, his senses alert to the special dangers impressed upon him by the Maharal's chanted instructions. Above the hubbub of the street sounds he heard the cry of a child gasping for breath. No matter what the cause, the child must be saved.

Joseph pushed people aside as he crossed the cobblestone street and with big steps followed the baby's cry to the second story of a dwelling house. In ragged swaddling clothes lay an infant unable to breathe because of congestion in his nose and throat. His mother and father stood by, grief-stricken, expecting death and unable to help.

Lifting the baby to him, the Golem breathed great gusts of air into his mouth. Then he heated some water in the fireplace and steamed the child's throat until it was clear and the baby breathed easily. The Golem first drew the baby closer to him, and then hastily put him in the arms of his father. Without waiting to be thanked, he hurried into the darkness outside.

"No child must die during the Passover period or else

the Jews will be blamed and tortured." This was the Golem's understanding.

The night before Passover, Joseph the Golem neared the end of his watch over the city of Prague. At midnight the task entrusted to him would be completed and the terrible responsibility put upon him would end.

Suddenly his sensitive nose picked up the smell of fire, and looking up he saw smoke curling in the distance toward the River Moldau. He pushed by the people in the marketplace and with long strides reached a knoll beside the riverbank. On this hill he saw the Children's Home burning. The caretakers were trying in vain to extinguish the fire, carrying small buckets of water from the river.

Immediately Joseph the Golem took a barrel in each hand and carried two barrels of water at a time from the river to the home on the bluff, then back again to the river. Back and forth he went with incredible speed.

When the fire was under control, Joseph the Golem made of clay took every child from his crib or bed. He dressed them all and placed them on the grass by the river to breathe the fresh air. Soon they stopped their whimpering and their caretakers regained composure. Still the Golem lingered, patting a girl's curly hair and playing with a restless boy. From one child to another went the Golem, bringing food and drink, tending to each one's needs.

The Golem appeared to have forgotten the mission entrusted to him. These children, saved at his hands from death by fire, no longer needed him; yet he stayed to comfort them.

In his slaughtering house on the outskirts of Prague, John the rich slaughterer still waited for a child to die so he could accuse the Jews of child murder and organize a bloody attack on the Jewish quarter. This night before Passover was his last chance.

It happened that on a small farm not far from John's slaughtering house, the farmer's child took sick and died. This was John's opportunity. He placed the body of the dead child inside the carcass of a slaughtered pig and put it in his wagon. Then he started toward the Jewish quarter of Prague, where he planned to deposit it on the lawn of the Synagogue for the city night watchman to find.

The road from John's house wound past the Children's Home on the Moldau River, where the Golem was busily tending the orphans of Prague. Joseph's sensitive nose and sharp ears picked up the scent of death and the sound of the carriage wheels as it approached. With a last look at the children, he slowly walked to the road, then quickened his steps as his mission came closer.

The carriage reached him. He stopped it by putting his body in the way of the horses, who reared up in fear. Joseph reined them in and examined the inside of the carriage.

When he saw the child's dead body in the carcass of the pig, his mystical instructions told him just what to do. He tied John the slaughterer with strong rope to the pig's carcass containing the child's dead body. At dawn, he deposited the entire bundle on the lawn of the Rathaus, the city hall of Prague.

In the morning when the city council members came to the Rathaus, the mystery of the child murder accusations was cleared up forever. John was forced to confess that year after year he had used the natural deaths of infants to fan hatred to the point of attack and murder of innocent citizens.

The city of Prague had become safe. The Golem's work was done.

With long steps the mechanical man walked past the Synagogue where the Maharal was waiting for him, over the cobbled streets of Prague, through the archways of the city gates and out into the countryside toward the River Moldau. He headed for the Children's Home of Prague, where lived the orphans whom he had saved from death by fire. There he stayed to help care for the children.

The Maharal was perplexed when the Golem did not return that Passover day. Eight days of Passover passed, and still there were no signs of Joseph the Golem.

When the festival was over, the Maharal went out in search of his creature who had, through mystical powers, performed miracles for the Jews of Prague. He finally found him in the Children's Home on the knoll near the River Moldau, working quietly with the children, tending gently to their needs.

"Return to your bench in the Synagogue!" commanded the Maharal.

Joseph continued what he was doing.

"Golem! Leave these children and come back with me to the Synagogue where you belong," ordered the Rabbi firmly.

The Golem worked on. He neither looked up nor paid the slightest attention to his master.

The Maharal understood that his power alone was no longer strong enough to control the Golem, who had become devoted to these children and had developed a will of his own to serve them. The Rabbi knew how dangerous a mechanical man could become if he had no master and would obey no one. The instructions of the Cabala had not prepared the Maharal of Prague for this moment of crisis.

Then the Maharal remembered the parchment that he had inserted in the clay Golem's forehead to bring him to life and action on the bank of the Moldau. The mystical word on this parchment had given the clay man understanding of his purpose in Prague. Now that this purpose was accomplished, the parchment must be removed.

As Joseph bent over a small boy's crib, the Maharal reached for his forehead and pulled out the parchment.

At once the Golem turned and walked stiffly and dumbly out the door, throwing over furniture that was in his way. He broke through the gate of the Children's Home and ran madly toward the central city. There he clattered through the stone streets, treading on people and animals who did not run from his path. He tore up street lamps and smashed carriages and wagons.

The Maharal ran after the Golem, trying to stop his destructive actions with mystical incantations. Joseph did not heed him but ran amok in a crazy zigzag path through the city. When he reached the Synagogue, he stopped short, walked slowly up the steps, pushed the heavy door open, and sat down on his bench, mute and motionless as he had been before.

His spirit gone, Joseph the Golem became again the mechanical man who responded only to human command.

That night, the Maharal said to Joseph the Golem, "Don't sleep on the bench in the House of Judgment tonight. Go up to the attic of the Synagogue and make your bed there!"

Joseph obeyed the Maharal's order. He walked slowly up the narrow winding staircase and fell asleep on the wooden floor under the eaves of the roof.

After midnight, the Maharal called his son-in-law Isaac and his student Jacob, who had helped him create the Golem, and said, "I have called you to tell you that the Golem is no longer needed."

The three men, the Maharal, his son-in-law, and his student, went up to the attic and looked at their friend the Golem. They took opposite positions to the ones they had taken when they created him. They stood at his head and gazed into his now familiar and dear face.

They circled him, beginning from left to right, seven times each, chanting formulas from the Cabala. When they had finished, the Golem was again a huge clay figure.

The men took off his clothes, wrapped him in prayer shawls, and finally covered him with pages of old prayer books, so that he was hidden from sight.

The Maharal sent out an edict forbidding everybody to go up to the attic of the Synagogue.

Nobody did go up to look at the Golem. He is probably still lying there, buried deep under pages of old prayer books.

# 7

# THE BORROWER
## Jewish Version

A silversmith lived not far from a miserly rich man, over the mountain and in the very next valley, past wavy wheat fields that moved like an ocean in the warm summer wind.

The two men hardly knew each other until one day the silversmith climbed up the mountain and down the valley, by the golden fields, to the rich man's sumptuous home to borrow a large silver spoon. Then he climbed back up the hill and down again into his own valley, carrying the lovely handwrought spoon with him.

A few days later, in the heat of the summer, he ascended the very same hill, and passed the wavy wheat fields to the rich man's home in the grove of cool eucalyptus trees. Wiping the sweat from his brow, the borrower returned the spoon and with it a tiny silver spoon that resembled it in every detail except its size.

"But I lent you only one spoon," protested the rich man.

"Your lovely spoon," replied the borrower, "gave birth to this tiny spoon. The mother and child rightfully are yours. Therefore I am returning them both to you."

Disbelieving but pleased, the greedy rich man smiled with delight at his good fortune and accepted the two silver spoons in place of the one.

Some weeks later, the silversmith ascended the mountain again and made the descent past the lush, vibrant wheat fields to the home of the rich man in the eucalyptus grove. This time he requested the loan of a large silver goblet, which the rich man readily granted him.

In a few days, the silversmith trudged back past vale and dale to return the costly handwrought goblet, and with it, a tiny goblet, identical in every respect except size.

"Your goblet," he explained to the rich man, "gave birth to this lovely little one. I'm returning them because both rightfully belong to you."

Again delighted, the greedy rich man smiled and graciously accepted the goblet and its offspring.

For the third time the borrower went up the hot hill and down into the cool valley to the luxurious home of the rich man.

"Would you be kind enough to lend me your gold watch?" he asked.

"With pleasure," said the rich neighbor readily. Thinking of the lovely small watch he would receive as a gift from his generous neighbor, he lent his most elaborate watch, set in pearls and diamonds.

Many days passed by and the silversmith did not return the watch. After a while the rich man became impatient and worried about his pearl-and-diamond watch. He ordered his carriage and drove it past his wheat fields, up the mountainside, down the other side of the mountain to the home of the silversmith.

"I have come to inquire about my watch," he said politely.

The borrower sighed unhappily. "I was about to take the trip to tell you that your watch had died and that I was forced to bury it," he said.

"Died?!" shouted the rich man, enraged. "Since when can a watch die?"

"If you could believe that your silver spoon gave birth to a baby spoon," said the cunning borrower, "and that your silver goblet gave birth to a baby goblet, why are you so surprised that your watch died?"

And he turned to his work with a smile.

# 8

# DID THE TAILOR
# HAVE A NIGHTMARE?

Benjamin the tailor was seated at his sewing table, stabbing away with his needle at a heavy coat which had to be patched for the wood gatherer. The winter in Russia was starting early. The townspeople would need their wood, and the wood gatherer would need his coat.

"Everything depends on me," thought Benjamin the tailor with great satisfaction.

Except for a continuous backache which he accepted without complaint, he was a happy man. "Is there a tailor who doesn't have a backache?" he asked himself.

A smile crossed his face as he thought of his wife and children. How lucky he was to eke out a living for them! Not that they were rich, heaven forbid, but did they ever starve? There was white bread and fish on the table every Friday night—well, almost every. And that was more than other members of his community could boast.

And the war. That crazy Frenchman Napoleon had swept through the country with his great armies, but Benjamin's village had not suffered at all, at least no direct attacks. Perhaps it was too small and insignificant even to attract cannon balls. After all, Napoleon was a great man and maybe he couldn't be bothered. So nobody in the village even knew what a French soldier looked like. Benjamin felt warm and snug in his sewing room as his thoughts rambled on to the rhythm of his needle.

Rumors were spreading that Napoleon had suffered a great defeat in Moscow and was in flight across the cold, white country. "Good riddance to him. It will be a happy moment when he goes back to France," muttered the tailor contentedly.

His pleasant thoughts were interrupted by a blast of cold wind and gusts of snow as the door was pushed open by a short, stocky, almost bald man in a French soldier's uniform, bedecked with ribbons and medals.

The impressive military man cried out in fear, his voice shaking, "Save me! They want to kill me! Help me!"

The tailor asked no questions. A man in danger must be helped. So he said quickly, "Get into this bed! I'll cover you up and no one will find you!"

The foreign soldier obeyed, crawling quickly into the bed. The tailor spread a heavy red feather quilt over him, then threw a blue feather quilt over the first and a brown one over the second and a pink one over the third.

Was it hot under the pile of feather quilts? Well, there are times when even a great man in uniform with medals must sweat.

No sooner had the feather quilts settled than three Russian soldiers, armed with spears, burst through the door of the tailor's house. "Have you seen anyone running away? Has anyone come to your house?" they demanded. "Quick! Answer!"

"Who would come to my house except a customer?" queried the tailor, who was nobody's fool.

To make sure, the Russians searched the shop, piercing their spears into the closets and under the bed. Just before leaving, to make doubly sure, they plunged their spears several times through the four feather quilts. Then, out into the snowstorm they ran to continue their search.

The Frenchman stuck his head out from under the feather quilts. His face was white as the snow.

"Have they gone?" he asked.

"Yes," answered the tailor, "it's safe to come out."

The stranger jumped off the bed, straightened his short, stocky body to its greatest height, and pulling a feather out of his hair, said, "I am the Emperor Napoleon! You have saved me from death, and I shall repay you."

What other tailor in all history has been in such a plight? Benjamin stood there, silent as a grave. Napoleon himself was speaking!

"I wish to grant you three wishes. Ask for three things, and you shall have them," continued the Emperor. "But speak quickly. Do you understand? Any three things your heart desires."

What a situation! Napoleon was offering him three wishes. Napoleon himself!

Benjamin stood silent, twisting his beard. What should he ask for? He remained deep in thought for several moments.

Finally he muttered, "My roof has been leaking in several places for many years, Your Majesty, and I must set up pots to catch the rain. It would be a great relief to have a snug roof on rainy days. Would it be possible, Your Highness, to have my roof fixed?"

Napoleon looked down at the little tailor, smiling. "Very well! Your roof shall be mended! Now ask again, quickly. Remember, only two more things."

Benjamin stroked his beard and twisted his sideburns while he thought. How hard—poor man that he was—to think of anything he needed! He was satisfied with his work, his wife, his children, with life itself. What should he want? Finally, he had an idea.

He ventured thoughtfully, "My wife and I have been married for thirty years and we are growing old. When was the last time she had a new dress? I can't even remember when. Please, Your Majesty, order a new dress for my wife. This will make her very happy for the rest of her days."

"Very well," said Napoleon, trying to hide his smile. "Your roof will be mended and your wife will have a new dress. And you have another wish. I am Napoleon the

Emperor and you can ask me for anything. Just one more wish, and make it a good one!"

Poor Benjamin! With a mended roof and a new dress for his wife, he could think of nothing more he needed. As usual when he thought deeply, he twisted his sideburns.

"Do I—do I have to ask for something?" he blurted out. He was afraid of offending the Emperor, who stood there, at attention, his short body stretched to its greatest height, looking down at him.

"I said three wishes, and three wishes it must be," ordered Napoleon.

"I—I," stammered the humble tailor, "I really cannot think of anything else I need. But if I must have a third wish, may I ask you to answer a question? I would really like to know: How did you feel when the Russians drove their spears through the feather quilts?"

Napoleon's anger was terrible to see. "How dare you?" he shouted. "For your boldness, I order you shot to death."

Before the bewildered tailor could say another word, the emperor called his soldiers. The poor tailor was bound and dragged like a lifeless bundle out of his shop.

"Where are you taking me? What will happen to me? What about my wife and children?" he pleaded.

"What's the use of all your questions?" grumbled the guards grimly. "This is your last night on earth. Tomorrow morning you will be put to death."

All night long, Benjamin the tailor prayed and wept and remembered his sins and wept again. One look at the night guards and he knew he could expect no mercy from them.

At dawn, he was tied to a tree. A group of soldiers stood at attention, ready, their guns loaded. An officer waited with a watch in his hand while the seconds ticked away.

The terrified tailor, pale and trembling in every limb, could hardly stand up. He felt the perspiration oozing down his body. One second he was hot, the next he was cold. How else would a tailor feel facing a firing line of soldiers of the French army?

The officer finished counting the seconds. In clipped tones, he ordered the soldiers, "When I say *one*, lift your guns; *two*, aim at the wretch's head; *three*, fire."

The group stood ready for the moment of death.

"One!" said the officer.

The soldiers lifted their guns.

"Two!" said the officer.

They aimed at the tailor's head.

Before the officer could say "three," there was a thundering sound of horses' hooves and a corps of Napoleon's men galloped to a sudden stop.

"Don't shoot!" shouted the leader.

He led his horse toward the tailor and addressed him softly. "The Emperor Napoleon grants you a pardon. His Royal Highness asks me to deliver this letter to you."

The tailor, more dead than alive, opened the letter with shaking hands, and read, "You wanted to know how I felt under the feather quilts. Now you know. I felt exactly as you feel now."

The tailor took a long breath, wiped his forehead, wrapped himself in his coat, and walked home through the cold and snow.

# Tales about Chelm, the City of Fools

# 9

# WHO AM I?

Chelm was the city of fools. There are many fools in this world, and you must have met some of them, but these were different from any fools you have ever known.

For example, they were all interested in scholarly problems, such as "Which is more important, the sun or the moon?"

So they brought this question to the Rabbi, the greatest Chelmite of them all, who put his finger to his head, stroked his beard slowly, and thought it all through carefully before he answered, "Why, the moon of course! Does it not shine at night, when it is needed? The sun shines only during the day, when it is light anyway, and there is no need for it at all!"

Could any explanation be clearer?

Once the Rabbi was spending the night at an inn with some of his students. One of the students had to make an early train. He asked the innkeeper to wake him at dawn.

The next morning it was pitch dark when the innkeeper roused him from the deepest slumber. Careful not to disturb the sleeping Rabbi, the student groped in the darkness for his clothes. By mistake, he put on the Rabbi's long black gabardine gown.

As he hurried through the cold streets to make the train,

he wrapped his cloak about him for protection, never noticing the error he had made. Remembering the Rabbi's explanation, he thanked the moon for taking the trouble to light the way for him. When he arrived at the station, the pious student stopped short before his own reflection in the station mirror. He stared at the long black priestly gown.

"What an idiot that innkeeper is!" he exclaimed in anger. "I asked him to wake me, and instead he woke the Rabbi!"

The problem of keeping track of one's identity generally troubled the Chelmites. "Who am I?" was a question they faced constantly, especially on Fridays when they went to the public baths to cleanse themselves to greet the Sabbath. They were convinced that people would be taken for each other were it not for their clothing, which set them apart. Otherwise, weren't all men created alike?

Herschel the baker was especially afraid that he would get lost when he shed his clothes in the bathhouse. He feared he would never again be able to discover who he really was. He might be taken for Yosele the shoemaker and have to spend the rest of his days at a cobbler's bench, or Moshe the water carrier and be obliged to carry heavy skins of water through cold, early-morning streets, or Yitzchak the roofer and broil for the rest of his days on hot roofs. How would he ever prove he was Herschel the baker and belonged in the heavenly heat of his bakery? He might lose his rights to the mouth-watering smells of his rising yeast-dough bread and his wonderful almond cake.

This possibility began to frighten him so much that he resolved to find a foolproof way to avoid it. He stroked his beard thoughtfully, and finally a good idea came to him. To make perfectly clear who he was, the baker tied a red string around his right leg. This would be proof positive that he really was Herschel the baker. "Now I am safe!" he assured himself. "Now I can never be taken for anybody else."

Sure enough, every time he looked down he saw proof of his identity. There was the red string around his right leg, and he felt sure of himself. He could get dressed and next Monday enter his bakery with the assurance that he would know what to do with the big bags of flour and the packages of butter and almonds.

Then, one Friday afternoon, a terrible thing happened. Herschel the baker was undressing in preparation for his Sabbath bath. Before he took off his last piece of clothing, he carefully tied a red string around his right leg. Yes, there was the string in full view, proving that he was who he thought he was, namely Herschel the baker. Nobody could fool him!

He took his bath and came out feeling warm and clean and happy. He had never before felt so content. He pinched himself to make sure it was really he who felt so good. Ouch! He did feel the pinch, but to make doubly sure, he looked for the red string, for that would be proof beyond doubt.

Alack and alas! The red string was no longer there. Perhaps it had loosened and fallen off. Without it, he was no longer sure of himself.

To add to the confusion, a man he had never seen before, a stranger to Chelm, had a red string on *his* leg. Perhaps he had found Herschel's string and decided to use it to keep track of who *he* was. What a mix-up!

The baker panicked. Now that the worst had happened and somebody else had the red string on his leg, Herschel thought, "If that man is really me, who then am I?

"Friend," said the unhappy baker to the man with the red string on his leg, "I have never seen you before, but I know who you are. You are I, Herschel the baker. And now that I have told you who you are, please be good enough to tell me who I am, so that I may know where to go and what to do."

# 10

# GOLDEN SHOES

The question of who is who and what is what became a matter of utmost importance when the Chelmites decided that for a community like theirs it was important to have a Chief Sage. It was not enough to have a Council of Sages because Chelm seemed to have deeper problems than most cities. So they held an election and elected a Chief Sage.

To their great disappointment, however, nobody paid any attention to the Chief Sage as he walked out on the street. Why, he looked the same as any other Chelm citizen! How could they set him apart so everybody would know he was the Chief Sage of Chelm? They put their heads together in council, for in Chelm ideas always came up when heads were put together.

After a few minutes, the solution came. What else but a pair of golden shoes would do it? Who but a Chief Sage in Chelm would wear golden shoes? So the Chief Sage was given golden shoes to wear.

"Now everybody will know that he is Chief Sage," they reasoned.

The Chief Sage put on his golden shoes and strutted proudly onto the street. As luck would have it, rain had been falling for days, and the mud was deep. As he sloshed in the mire, head high, he looked around for respectful glances. To his dismay, nobody looked his way. He was being ignored! Nobody paid attention to him.

He looked down at the golden shoes. They were covered with thick mud and didn't look golden at all.

The Chief Sage complained bitterly, "If I don't get respect quickly, I'll resign!"

"You're perfectly right," said the sages of Chelm. "We must do something about it immediately."

Again they put their heads together, each with his finger pointed to his forehead this time. They pondered and discussed, discussed and pondered. As always, an idea came. They decided to order for their Chief Sage a pair of fine leather shoes to wear over the golden shoes. Thus the golden shoes would be protected!

Sure enough, when the Chief Sage went into the street, the leather shoes protected the golden shoes from the mud. He walked along, head high, on the alert for admiring glances. But since no one even got a peek at the golden shoes, how could they tell it was the Chief Sage and show him respect?

Again he complained. "What's the use of being Chief Sage in the city of Chelm if nobody knows of your high office?"

"You're right," agreed the sages. "We must think of something to make you stand out."

Again they went into council, heads together in a thoughtful circle, fingers to forehead, and this time eyes closed for greater concentration. The idea came in a burst! They ordered a new pair of leather shoes for the Chief Sage, to be worn over the golden shoes for protection. This time, however, the leather shoes had holes in them to allow the gold to shine through.

Out walked the Chief Sage, head high, his eyes searching for recognition and respect. Again he was disappointed. People passed him by without a glance.

Looking down, he saw that the mud had oozed through the holes and muddied up the golden shoes as well as the leather shoes.

The Chief Sage was furious and threatened to resign.

"I'm humiliated," he complained. "How can I walk out on the street unnoticed?"

What should be done about it? There seemed no way out of this dilemma.

However, the sages had hope. Again they put fingers to heads and heads together; they closed their eyes and even furrowed their foreheads in deepest concentration.

Sure enough, as if with one mind, the idea came!

They scurried about to find straw, a little from this mattress and a little from that one, until there was enough to stuff into the holes in the leather shoes. This did prevent the mud from muddying the golden shoes, but the old problem remained. Nobody could get a glimpse of the golden shoes. How then could they recognize the worth of the Chief Sage and show him respect?

This was the last straw! The Chief Sage was beside himself, enraged, beard and kaftan flying. The Chelm sages were desperate.

Again, fingers went to heads and heads went together, eyes closed, foreheads furrowed, and left hands stroked beards. As always, the Chelmites were triumphant. Not for naught did they have a reputation for their unique brand of wisdom.

"From now on," they told the Chief Sage, "you will walk out on the street wearing ordinary leather shoes. But, in order to stand out as our Chief Sage and get the respect due you, you will wear the golden shoes—one on the left hand and one on the right hand."

The Chief Sage followed their suggestion. As he walked around the city of Chelm with the golden shoes on his hands, the citizens craned their necks to stare at him. He was certainly attracting attention! Now the citizens knew who he was. He was delighted.

# 11

# LET'S STEAL THE MOON

The people of Chelm loved their city and tried to improve it in every way. Whenever they heard of something new and different in another city, they wanted it for themselves. What is good for others is good for us, they reasoned.

Imagine how excited they became when they learned that in some towns the streets were lighted at night. What a brilliant idea! With street lamps there would be no need to stumble in the dark or to come right up to a person and peer closely into his face to recognize him, or guess when you came to a street corner, or lose your way because you made a wrong turn. A wonderful improvement, lamps in the streets! Why hadn't they thought of this before?

As was the custom, all the citizens of Chelm came together to discuss the appealing new notion of installing lights on their street corners.

As they sat in council, thinking the matter through, a white-bearded patriarch stood up and spoke, "Streetlights, my friends, would cost us a great deal of money and where would the money come from? From our fund for the poor? That is forbidden!

"On the other hand, there is a luminary up in the sky that helps us for part of the month and leaves us in the dark for part of the month. There are nights when the moon shines and Chelm has enough light. There are other nights when there is no moon and Chelm is dark. Now, why can't the moon shine for us every night?"

"Why not?" wondered the people of Chelm, looking skyward and shaking their heads thoughtfully.

Then they drew closer to the old man, delighting in his great wisdom as he unfolded his plan. The wise patriarch persuaded the people of Chelm to wait for a night when the moon was large and full, shedding light into every nook and cranny of their dark streets. Then, to put it simply and directly, they would steal the moon and guard her safely until the dark nights of the month, when they would hang her in the skies to light up their streets.

"Steal the moon? Why not?" reasoned the people of Chelm, rubbing their chins in deepest contemplation.

Gimpel, who always had the most advanced ideas, suggested, "While we have it down, why not clean and polish it so that it will be brighter than ever?"

"Polish the moon? Why not?" agreed the people of Chelm, bewildered by the onrush of their own creative ideas.

They had no difficulty at all in capturing the moon. It was a simple matter. They filled a barrel with water and left it open, exposed to the moon's light. Then ten Chelmites stood ready with sackcloth.

The moon, unaware of the plot, moved into the barrel of water. When it was clearly trapped, the Chelmites covered the barrel with the heavy sackcloth and bound it down with thick strong rope. To make certain that everything was as it should be, they put the official seal of Chelm on the barrel and carried it carefully into the synagogue where it would be safe from all harm. They checked every night to make sure the seal was not broken.

After two weeks, the nights became very dark and again they began to bump into each other on the streets, bruise their shins, and lose their way because of wrong turns in the darkness.

This was the time! They sent word through the town, and the people gathered to help take the moon out of the barrel and hang it in the sky. They were confident that, with all their minds working on the problem, there would be a way of hoisting it up and securing it there. They knew it was possible, for hadn't they seen the moon up there month after month? Besides, they had collected all the ladders in Chelm and tied them together end to end in preparation for this moment.

Polishing cloths were also gathered in a gigantic heap in front of the synagogue, where the important event would take place. The women of Chelm vied with each other for positions from which they could help in the polishing.

Then came the moment they had been planning for. They uncovered the barrel carefully, squinting their eyes so that they would not be blinded by the brilliance of the moon's light.

They opened their eyes wide. Their moon was gone! How could that be? They looked at each other in utter confusion.

Who could have released their moon, securely trapped in a water barrel and sealed by the official seal of the city of Chelm? Surely no Chelmite could have done it! Bandits? Marauders from a neighboring town? But the seal remained unbroken! They shook their heads and looked skyward, deeply disturbed by this mysterious happening.

One thing they were sure of. Had they set proper guards over their moon, it would have remained safe and they would have found a way to hang it in the sky. Far from being discouraged, they were confident that they would know how to do it next time.

# Folktales Told
# by Immigrants
# to Israel after
# World War II:
# Folk Festival
# in Sedot Mikhah

# FOREWORD

The stories in this section of the book are, in a way, a continuation of the tales you have just finished reading. However, they belong to a different ethnopoetic (folk-literary) genre. Unlike the earlier stories, which stemmed from literary or written tradition, the tales that follow come from oral sources. They were transmitted by storytellers to listening audiences rather than by books to readers.

In 1970 when her work first came to my attention, I became interested in Dr. Serwer-Bernstein, because I saw in her a gifted American narrator of Jewish folktales for children. I was delighted to find that there was someone in the United States spinning traditional Jewish stories in her own individual style for young readers.

I invited Dr. Serwer-Bernstein to visit with my students at the Hebrew University. The encounter of this American author with my Hebrew University students was most profitable, an inspiring event for both sides.

After a while, our guest asked my permission to browse in the Israel Folktale Archives, and this was readily granted. In 1970, there were about ten thousand folktales in the archives, and Dr. Serwer-Bernstein joined the students and scholars sifting through the IFA for folktales from the oral tradition in Israel. Some of these stories, selected by Dr. Serwer-Bernstein and rewritten in her own elegant style, are included in the following section.

The IFA had been established in 1955 when I returned to the Hebrew University in Jerusalem after completing my graduate studies in folklore, anthropology, and comparative literature at Indiana University.

Following my studies with Professor Stith Thompson, the renowned author of the *Motif Index of Folk Literature*, I realized that there were no authentic, genuine collections of Jewish folktales originating from oral tradition. Many Jewish communities, especially in Asia and Africa, had no printing presses at their disposal, and their folktales were transmitted exclusively by oral tradition.

On the other hand, in those communities where Hebrew letter printing presses were available (mainly in Europe and other Jewish Ashkenazi centers), many of the printed folktale collections consisted of stories strongly censored and changed by their editors to fit the normative ideological and religious worldview of the Jewish establishment.

How were we to set up a system for collecting stories in the early 1950s, when thousands of new immigrants were arriving every year? They were arriving on the "wings of eagles" from three continents, Europe, Africa, and Asia, speaking many different languages, and belonging to over seventy distinct Jewish ethnic groups and subgroups. It seemed logical to get to these storytellers as soon as possible after their arrival.

We tried to locate the narrators in each group. At the same time, we had to train collectors who could win the confidence of the storytellers and record their stories in the original language or in a faithful Hebrew translation.

With the help of folklore students as well as of volunteers interested in their own cultural folk heritage, we set up a national network of narrators and collectors. This network still exists today and is the method of folktale collecting in Israel. Thanks to all these efforts, we now have close to eighteen thousand orally transmitted folktales in the IFA, which is located at Haifa University.

Who were the collectors? A survey of the 100 collectors

active in 1970 indicates that the group was heterogeneous. It included journalists and scholars, merchants and house- wives, nurses and teachers. There were men and women, Jews, Arabs, and Druzes. It should be mentioned that 600 of the 18,000 IFA folktales stem from non-Jewish ethnic groups in Israel.

At the very beginning of the project, we decided to bring together the outstanding raconteurs and collectors once a year for a storytelling festival. We hoped that they would enjoy each other's tales and experience the sense of par- ticipation in an important, mutually satisfying effort to pre- serve their respective cultural pasts.

These annual daylong events usually took place in a *moshav*, or settlement, in the southern Judean foothills, called Sedot (Fields of) Mikhah, named after the Hebrew writer Mikhah Josef Berdczewski (1865-1921). This writer, also known by his pen name Bin Gorion, had dealt more than any other Hebrew writer of his generation with Jew- ish folk-narrative, especially with rabbinic legends of the oral tradition. His *Mimekor Israel* (From the Source of Israel) contains a collection of 930 Hebrew stories, most of them from printed sources. His book was translated into English (three volumes) and published by Indiana University Press. In 1990, the same press published a one-volume paperback edition of 113 tales selected from Bin Gorion's monumen- tal work.

When Dr. Serwer-Bernstein discussed with me the set- ting of her new book, we decided to place it right in the midst of one of the folklore festivals in Sedot Mikhah. Each nar- rator would stand up and tell a story from his or her coun- try of origin.

There were no prizes: it was not a contest in that sense. Every narrator received a thank-you souvenir and felt re- warded by it and the sheer fact that his or her ethnic folk heritage was becoming part of the pluralistic folk culture of Israel.

The sessions were conducted in Hebrew, the common

language among them. Although many of the narrators, recent immigrants, told their tales in broken Hebrew, the plots, contents, and messages of the tales were preserved. "Don't look at the jar, but at what is within it" is an old saying of the Hebrew sages, and a Jewish folktale is no exception.

One may wonder why there are two stories in this book involving the moon. Let me try to explain.

Some of the narrative motifs and images in folktales are universal, and some are specifically ethnic. The moon is a universal image, but it plays a specific role in the Jewish folk tradition.

The Jewish calendar is lunar. The Jewish year cycle (the Shabbat, the festivals, and related rites) is based on the moon. No wonder that there exists, in addition to the religious monthly prayer of sanctification of the moon, secular songs and legends focused on it. In many of them, the moon is the symbol of the people of Israel; in the Messianic age, it will return to its original size, equal to that of the sun. The moon is also the symbol of beauty, dignity, and modesty.

It is not always possible to trace the origin of a folktale. But we do know that the first story told at the festival, "Clothing the Moon," stems from a short parable of the great eighteenth-century hasidic Rabbi Nachman of Bratslav, grandson of the Rabbi Israel Baal Shem Tov (Besht), the founder of Hasidism.

Rabbi Nachman of Bratslav has been compared by folktale scholars to Hans Christian Andersen. The stories told by both have become folklorized and constitute an integral part of both the ethnic (Jewish and Danish, respectively) and universal folk heritage.

Dov Noy

# DEAR READERS

There are two pictures in my imagination from my early discussions with Professor Noy about the setting of the following stories.

The first picture is of a group of students from the Folklore Department of the Hebrew University waiting at Ben Gurion Airport outside Tel Aviv for the arrival of a plane carrying new immigrants to Israel. It may be coming from Northern Africa or Asia if the newcomers have left Jewish communities of countries like Morocco, Yemen, Persia, Turkey, Afghanistan, Ethiopia, and Libya. Or the plane may be arriving from Europe if the newcomers are emigrating from countries like Germany, the Netherlands, Hungary, Poland, and Russia.

The plane lands. The ramp is lowered. The people, their faces aglow with excitement, step down gingerly, holding on to the railing, carrying children and small packages. They are dressed in many-colored garments, their heads covered with traditional scarves or turbans.

The students greet them warmly, "*Shalom, chaverim! Shalom, chaverim!*" (Hello, comrades.) They burst into song with the same words,

"*Shalom, chaverim,
Shalom, chaverim,*

*Shalom, shalom.*
*Shalom, chaverim,*
*Shalom, chaverim,*
*Shalom, shalom.*

"*B'ruchim haba'im! B'ruchim haba'im! B'ruchim haba'im!*"
(Welcome, newcomers!)

And then, leading them to a large circle of chairs, the students burst into another song:

"*Hineh, mah tov umah na'im*
*Shevet achim gam yachad.*
*Hineh, mah tov umah na'im*
*Shevet achim gam yachad!*"
(*"How good and how pleasant it is*
*For brothers to live together."*)

With tears in their eyes, the new immigrants join in the singing as well as they can. The students serve tea and cookies and join the group in the large circle.

As they drink, eyes shining through the emotions everybody is feeling, one student asks, "Who is your storyteller?"

Every planeload, from whatever country, has its traditional storyteller. The man or woman who comes forward is usually of the older generation, often dressed in multicolored native costume. Sometimes there are several storytellers in the group.

Without knowing how important their role has been, these gifted people have preserved the heritage of Jewish folklore in a great many languages and in the idioms of the many countries from which they have come. As they spin their yarns in the airport, the stories are recorded for the first time so that they can be preserved in the Israel Folktale Archives for future generations to enjoy.

Soon the newcomers feel free enough to get up, push back their chairs, and, singing their traditional melodies, perform folk dances. These songs and dances are recorded on video. The cinematography is not great, but the pictures are exciting anyway. You can see them in the Israel Folktale Archives in Haifa when you go to Israel.

And now there is another picture I have to imagine, since I was not there to experience it. Again, I invite you to join me in my fantasy.

It is of a storytelling festival that actually did take place once a year in Sedot Mikhah, a *moshav ovdim*, or workers' settlement, in southern Judea. Here the narrators came together to share tales and enjoy the great variety of colorful plots and narrative styles.

Imagine such a festival. Hundreds of people have gathered in Sedot Mikhah. They sit in a natural amphitheater, some in colorful native costumes, some in informal leisure clothes. They come from all parts of Israel, some to tell stories, some just to listen.

The stories are told in Hebrew, the only language shared by all the narrators. Because they are recent immigrants, Hebrew is difficult for them. Many of them do not speak fluently, but everybody listens with interest and applauds with enthusiasm. Each storyteller stands up and tells a tale stemming from his or her own country of origin, sometimes pointing out its relevance to the previous tale from another country.

As you read the stories in this section, try to relive such a storytelling event. I have written the tales in my own fashion for young readers and older ones who can still believe in gossamer cloth made of moonbeams, in a princess who is placed in the sky as the morning star, and in a boy who can outwit the devil.

As Professor Noy mentioned in the preceding foreword, the moon figures prominently in two stories in this book. Although the moon is a universal motif in folklore, it has special meaning for the Jews because of the Jewish lunar calendar. As they look up at the "man in the moon," they have traditionally thought him to be Joshua bin Nun, the disciple of Moses, who conquered ancient Canaan after the great leader's death.

No wonder that Nachman of Bratslav, one of the most imaginative of Jewish tale weavers, imposed on the tailors the task of fashioning a garment for the moon! How they accomplished this assignment is told in the first story in this section.

Now I invite you to join me at a folklore festival in progress on the rugged slopes of Sedot Mikhah.

# The Ukraine

# 12

# CLOTHING THE MOON

In our Ukrainian *shtetl* we had a wonderful storyteller. He did not tell of demons and witches, yet his tales had a magical quality. The people in his stories seemed to live in a mystical world made of gossamer and fairies' wings, where spiritual experiences were as commonplace as making *cholent* in your mother's oven.

I'm referring to Rabbi Nachman of Bratslav. He told short fragments of tales that were usually symbolic of lessons he wished to teach. But the stories themselves seem to sway in the breeze and glitter in the sunlight.

Talking of sunlight reminds me of one of his tales, which I would like to tell you. Perhaps I can embroider it a bit, just as his students did as they rethought and retold his beautiful ideas.

Once upon a time long ago, the moon became dissatisfied. She seemed to enjoy traveling in the dark sky at night like a queen among the surrounding stars. Yet she complained bitterly that she suffered from the cold of the night.

"Why can't I share the warmth of the day with the sun?" she asked.

The sun, to keep peace, promised her that he would have a garment woven that would keep her warm, especially during the cold winter nights. As you can imagine, this was not an easy promise to fulfill.

Who could help him in this difficult task? He thought first, of course, of the tailors, and he called the greatest of them together. The simple tailors, less well known, wanted to take part in this great undertaking, but they were not invited.

The great tailors met to plan how they would go about making a garment for the moon. Plan after plan was suggested, but nothing these famous tailors thought up would solve the problem of the changing size of the moon.

At the beginning of the month, as you know, the moon is a thin crescent, and it grows larger every night until it is a great big round full moon. Which of the moon's sizes should the tailors measure her for? They finally decided that the sun had assigned them an impossible task, and told him so.

At this point, the simple tailors stepped into the picture. They put their heads together, rubbed their beards, and twirled their sideburns as they thought of a solution to this difficult problem. How does even the best-intentioned of tailors sew a garment for a moon whose size is constantly changing?

They were about to give up when one of the poorest among them, Yankel by name, said in a low tone of voice, "Please, my friends, let us not give up. The moon must be kept content with her lot or she may decide not to serve us with her lovely light at night. What would we do then?"

Yankel, a humble man, looked down as he continued, "When I was a very little boy, I heard from my father, a learned man, about a kingdom very far away, I don't know where, known for its beautiful fabrics. The most famous of these has the substance of light and stretches or shrinks according to the size of what it has to cover. Wouldn't this fabric be just the thing for the moon's garment?"

"Of course!" they all shouted at once. "This wonderful fabric is just what we need!"

Since Yankel had brought them the news of this fabulous kingdom, they all agreed that he should set out immediately to find it and bring back the fabric made of light.

But what about money for the journey and for the cost of the material? The best they could do was to contribute a few kopeks each and wish Yankel luck.

You must be pitying this simple tailor with nothing but a few kopeks in his pocket and a half dozen loaves of bread in a bag given to him by his friend the local baker. You also must be wondering how he would go about finding a far-away, unknown land reputed to have a fabric made of light that could stretch and shrink according to the size of the moon as it waxed and waned in its monthly travels in the sky.

Well, that was exactly what the people he met along the way thought when he asked them for directions. They looked at him in wonderment and decided that he was either a fool or a crazy man. Many of them simply laughed in his face, turned their backs on him, and went about their work.

Yankel traveled for more than a year, sleeping under the stars and the moon. One very cold night, hungry and tired, he felt discouraged and thought of giving up and going home. Just then the moon seemed to shiver with cold, and he knew he would never abandon the search until he found the kingdom with the magic fabric.

One day Yankel reached the shore of a very wide river. Should he cross to pursue his search? Perhaps the ferry ride would take him in the wrong direction.

Discouraged, he sought the advice of the ferryman. To Yankel's delight, this was the first person who did not laugh at him. When asked the location of a kingdom where the tailor could find fabric made of light that would stretch or shrink with the size of the wearer, he simply gave the directions.

That is how Yankel the tailor finally found his way to the kingdom of lovely fabrics. When he arrived at the capital city, he was surprised to see how sad all of the people looked.

"Why is everybody in your beautiful city so sorrowful?" he inquired of a fruit dealer on a street corner.

"You must be a newcomer to our land," replied the dealer. "Otherwise you would know what we all know, that we are grieving because our Queen is grieving."

"Why, then, is your Queen so sorrowful?" asked Yankel.

Fighting back tears, the man answered, "Our Queen is despondent because her ceremonial dress, woven of light by our expert weavers, is unraveling. How can she go to her daughter's wedding? And how can the Princess be married if her mother is not at the wedding? Everything has been delayed, and nobody knows for how long. Isn't that enough to make us sad?"

"But don't you have tailors in this land who can mend the royal robe?" asked Yankel, excited at the possibility that he might be helpful in this unhappy situation. Wasn't he a tailor, and weren't his customers poor, so that most of his work consisted of mending ragged clothing?

"Yes, of course we have tailors," answered the fruit dealer. "But none of them know how to weave fabric out of light. The Queen's beautiful dress was woven many years ago, when the art of weaving light was well known, but it has long since been forgotten.

"The exquisite royal gown was worn for centuries by all our queens, whatever their size, because this wonderful fabric shrank or stretched to fit every one of them perfectly. And now that we have lost the secret of weaving light, what are we to do? None of our tailors have the skill to make the necessary repairs. Do you wonder that we are sad for the Queen and the young Princess, who is very much in love and longs to be married?"

"I am a tailor," revealed Yankel, "and I am willing to try my hand at repairing the royal gown. I have been mending clothes for many years, you know."

To Yankel's surprise, the fruit dealer hurriedly closed his shop. He led Yankel straight to the palace, because the Queen had decreed that all tailors who entered the kingdom must be brought to her at once. They were her only hope, since all the native tailors had tried and failed.

The palace was magnificent. The humble Yankel had never before seen a building so splendid. He was frightened and overwhelmed as he stood before the gracious Queen, who said sadly, "I am very grateful to you for offering to repair my gown, but the material itself is unraveling. I feel hopeless because our secret of weaving fabric out of light was lost long ago."

"I'd like to try," offered Yankel. He had already realized that if he succeeded, he would be close to solving the problem of weaving a garment for the moon. He could hardly breathe from excitement. "May I see the gown? I think it would be a good idea for me to begin by examining the material."

The gown was brought to a room assigned to Yankel for his work. He studied the lovely fabric closely.

It was exquisite, soft as moonlight, with a gossamer sheen, and he could see how pliable it was. Yes, Yankel was certain that this fabric was entirely appropriate for the moon's garment ordered by the sun.

He examined the gown for hours. Time passed and night fell. As the darkness made it harder for him to see, he moved closer to the window. Soon, a full moon rose high in the sky and its bright light fell on Yankel and on the sheer fabric he was studying so closely.

Then a wonderful thing happened. As the moonlight shone on the gown, it began to glow, and Yankel saw a miracle take place before his eyes. The dress, which had been unraveling so that it could not be mended, began to be rewoven in the light of the moon. Yes, Yankel saw before his very eyes the weaving of light, the forgotten secret.

Then Yankel did a strange thing. He cut a small swatch of the fabric from the hem of the dress, and held it up in the light of the moon. To his utter amazement, he saw this tiny piece of fabric grow to twice, three times, in a short time to ten times its size. The light of the moon was actually being woven into fabric.

Yankel turned to look at the Queen's dress. The moonlight had continued all this time weaving the fabric and restoring the garment to its original beauty. By the time the moon had to make way for the sun and the morning star to dominate the sky, the Queen's noble robe had been completely rewoven.

When he brought it to her the next morning, the Queen was delighted. As she put it on, the dress immediately shrank to her size to fit her perfectly. There was no reason now to delay the Princess's wedding.

The Queen, in her joy, did not forget to thank Yankel and she offered him any reward he wanted. The happy tailor asked her for the piece of fabric he had clipped and watched grow in the moonlight. She of course agreed that he could take it with him. She also gave him more than enough gold for a comfortable trip home.

Now Yankel had traveled for more than a year to reach the kingdom. It would take him an equal number of months to retrace his steps.

All during that long trip home, he held his swatch of fabric up to the bright light of the full moon whenever it shone in the sky. And each time he did, the fabric grew ten times larger. By the time he reached his city, the material was immense, in fact fully large enough to fit the moon.

The simple tailors were delighted to see Yankel again, and overjoyed when they saw the exquisite fabric. They sat down immediately around a large table and together they sewed a garment for the moon, soft and glowing.

The sun was happy to keep his promise and provide warmth for her on wintry cold nights. Of course, the garment fitted perfectly, expanding when the moon was full and contracting gradually as it slivered down to a thin and graceful crescent.

Everybody in the town was happy, everybody except perhaps the great tailors, who had not had the imagination or the courage to try until they succeeded. They never did learn the secret discovered by Yankel, that the moon provides the light to create her own robe.

And by the way, since it fits so well, she is wearing the luminous, gently glowing garment to this very day. You can see it for yourself if you look up at the sky at any point in the moon's waxing and waning as she travels across the dark night sky.

# Russia

# 13

# MELODIES

In a very small town in Russia, a group of boys learned together with a teacher whom they called Rebbe. They studied all day long, sometimes into the night, and if the truth be told, they loved what they were doing, every minute of it. Their whole bodies were involved, since they moved rhythmically to their chanting of the text and its interpretation.

They studied *Mishnah*, an interpretation of biblical law, and *Gemara*, a commentary on *Mishnah*, also Rashi, an interpretation of it all. If you put it all together, you could simply say they were studying Talmud.

The unusual thing about it was that they were not using the original language of the Talmud, which was a combination of Hebrew and Aramaic. They chanted in Yiddish. The reason they did this was to avoid desecrating the holy language, Hebrew, which they called *Lashon Hakodesh*, or holy tongue.

They found it all very exciting and they did it with gusto in a singsong chant that was prescribed by tradition. For Avrom, who is the student-hero of this tale, the chief charm of the whole procedure was the chant, because it sounded to him like a melody, and his head was full of melodies.

Avrom had been called Avromchik by the Rebbe and his fellow students since his mother's death when he was not much more than a baby. It was a loving name, as well as a

diminutive one, because Avromchik was small, even as he
approached the advanced age of sixteen.

The most endearing thing about Avromchik was, as I
said before, that his head was full of melodies. He picked
up songs wherever he went and from whoever happened to
be singing. The birds were probably the greatest source of
tunes, as were the wind, the crickets, and the waterfalls.
Sometimes he learned a new melody from a visitor passing
through the town.

You see, Avromchik had never heard an opera or a concert, nor did he have a radio or a TV set. All of the tunes in
his head came from nature or from other human beings and
when he learned a new melody, he worked on it in his head
all week long so that he could have a new *nigun* on the
Sabbath.

That was because there was no learning on Shabbos,
the day set aside for rest from the work of the week. On the
day of rest, the students sang *z'miros*, traditional songs,
and Avromchik loved to have a new melody to make every
Sabbath a glorious experience. Wasn't *Shabbos Hamalkah*,
the Sabbath Queen, all aglow at being ushered in by *z'miros*,
especially the wordless tunes, the ones called *nigunim*, sheer
melody?

Everybody was good to Avromchik, some because he
was small and looked vulnerable, some because he was an
orphan, but most of all, they liked him because of the melodies in his head. These he shared with his fellow students
and the Rebbe every Saturday after the midday meal. He
had a lovely voice which remained true even though it was
in the process of changing from a childlike soprano to something deeper.

The meal following the synagogue services on Saturday
was the most enjoyable of the week because of the fresh
*challah*, the gefilte fish, and the chicken soup with noodles.
Besides, everybody beamed with pleasure, remembering the
prayer melodies they had sung in synagogue.

They chanted the long grace after the meal in unison,

except for certain parts, which were solos for the Rebbe. And then came the *z'miros* and the *nigunim*, the wordless songs that they all sang lustily. These melodies were often the most sprightly for dancing. The boys and their Rebbe enjoyed dancing wildly, flinging their arms and legs in all directions at once with abandon.

I think I have made it clear that Avromchik was liked by friends and teacher alike. It was not unexpected, then, that the Rebbe would think of him immediately when Rav Melnikov, the jacket manufacturer, who owned the only factory in town, came to the *yeshivah* to look for a husband for his daughter, Sarale.

"Rav Melnikov has a jacket factory. He's a rich man. Avromchik is a poor orphan," reasoned the Rebbe to himself. "The boy studies well and sings like a bird. I'm sure he won't find it hard to learn the jacket business."

To Mr. Melnikov the Rebbe declared decisively, "I have just the young man for you. He's a bit shy when he speaks, but not when he sings. Then he's like a songbird. Your daughter will like him, as we all do, I'm certain."

"The important thing," replied Mr. Melnikov, "is that he should be able to learn the jacket business. My daughter, Sarale, is an innocent young girl and will like any man I choose for her. But will this Avrom show some talent for buying goods, manufacturing and selling his product? Singing, that's fine. But business, that's the essence of the matter if he marries my Sarale."

"I'm sure he'll learn all aspects of your business if you are patient and teach him," urged the Rebbe. "Give it a try and you'll see I'm right."

Mr. Melnikov agreed to test Avrom by sending him to the city to buy some fabrics.

That is how Avrom happened to be walking alone early the next morning on the main road to the city with a hundred rubles in his pocket. His assignment was to buy black satin cloth for the jackets the men would wear on the occasion of his marriage to Sarale.

He had not as yet met her or even seen her, but he had shyly agreed, by nodding his head with eyes down, to be married to the daughter of the richest man in the village, even though he had never before even thought of marriage at all. He had been too busy humming the tunes he loved to sing on Shabbos.

And now, he was trudging along on the road to the city. Slung over his shoulder was a bag in which he had packed cheese, bread, and fruit.

The long walk would take the better part of a day. Avromchik looked forward to the many hours of listening to the sounds of the countryside, the rustle of the wind through the trees, the hum of the insects, and best of all, the songs of the birds.

What he did not expect was the sudden sound of a melody played on a shepherd's flute, a melody so lovely that it totally enveloped him and gave him a sense of excitement he had never felt before. He jumped over the stone wall on the side of the road and followed the sound of the flute. Before long, he saw a flock of peaceful sheep grazing on a lush meadow.

There, sitting in their midst on a rock, totally engrossed in guarding his animals, was their shepherd playing the most haunting melody Avromchik had ever heard. His head swam with its beauty, and he felt an uncontrollable urge to know the tune so that he could sing it on the next Sabbath. What pleasure it would give his fellow students and the Rebbe!

When the shepherd ended the song, Avrom approached him and invited him to break bread. As they ate cheese and bread, he pleaded in breathless excitement, "Please teach me the wonderful tune you have been playing on your flute. It is so beautiful, I just have to learn it."

The young shepherd boy smiled, pleased at the compliment and amused at the outpouring of enthusiasm for a simple melody he played to keep his sheep calm and content. Then he took a bite of apple and a sip of water.

Mistaking the shepherd's amused smile and his slowness in responding as reluctance to share his tune, Avromchik went on pleading, "Please, I'll pay you to teach me this entrancing melody. I must have it for my Sabbath *z'miros*."

"Well," quipped the shepherd with a teasing, mischievous look at the eager student, "if you must have it, I'll teach it to you for fifty rubles."

For the first time in his life, Avromchik actually had enough money in his pocket to pay for something he wanted with all his heart and soul. "Fifty rubles it is," he agreed.

Then he sat down next to the shepherd, who taught him the lilting melody until he could sing it perfectly. Very happy with his new tune, he handed over the fifty rubles. No price was too high for a melody that made you feel happy, indeed joyous enough to dance. Any *hasid* would tell you that!

He thanked the shepherd and went on his way toward the city, singing his new tune to be sure he would not forget it.

Soon the sun hung low in the sky, and Avrom thought it must be time for evening prayers. He faced east and, as usual, chanted the traditional melodies in his sweet, true voice.

Suddenly, he heard another tune wafting over the evening stillness, a livelier tune than the one he had just bought. It was so beautiful that he felt the joy of it through his entire body.

He rushed through his prayers and left his evening meal uneaten. Following the rhythmic sound of the flute music, he leaped over the stone fence again. Silhouetted against the purple western sky was another shepherd guarding his flock and soothing the animals with the sound of his exquisite melody.

Again, Avromchik was entranced by the melodic lilt of the flute music and the great joy it made him feel. He longed to have this tune too as his very own. He pleaded with the shepherd to teach him the melody.

This time, as if his transaction with the other shepherd had been overheard, the flutist said at once, "I'll be happy to teach you my song, but you will have to pay fifty rubles for it."

The happy student agreed at once. After all, he did have fifty rubles in his pocket, and what better use could he put it to? Still another exquisite melody to add to his *Shabbos nigunim*! What joy he would bring to his fellow students and to the Rebbe!

As soon as he had learned the tune to his satisfaction, he took the remaining fifty rubles from his pocket and gladly handed them to the shepherd. As they parted, he started to sing both melodies to make certain that he would remember them. To his delight, they sounded wonderful when sung in sequence.

"What a coincidence!" he thought. "These two melodies go hand in glove, like bread and butter, like raisins and almonds, like mother and child, like spider and web. They seem like two patterns that some artist wove into the same cloth, each to enhance the other."

The word *cloth* reminded Avrom of the errand he had been sent on. Cloth! He was to have bought cloth for the jackets to be worn at his wedding to Sarale, whom he did not even know and had never seen.

And now he did not have the money anymore. He was perfectly satisfied. Since he did not have the money, he no longer had to continue his journey because he could no longer buy satin for the wedding jackets. And since there would be no wedding jackets, there would be no wedding. Probably Mr. Melnikov would be furious that he had spent the jacket money on melodies, and would cancel the wedding anyway. Mr. Melnikov would surely look for another husband for his daughter, one with business in his head, not music, and Sarale would be happy with him.

No matter. All things considered, everything was turning out well. Most important, Avrom had two exquisite new melodies to sing on the Sabbath. Sooner or later, he would find another bride, and perhaps her father would be a *hasid* who would appreciate the songs Avrom brought back from the countryside. Perhaps his new father-in-law would even get to like the tunes in Avrom's head, as Mr. Melnikov never could have, since he had absolutely no music in his soul.

# *Iraq*

# 14

# A CONTEST
## Jewish Version

In the land where I was born, the rulers were so cruel that even the stories we told revealed that we did not feel safe among them. We liked to tell our children about the many ways we found to outwit the wicked plots against us, so that our community could live in peace.

One day not so very long ago, the Vizier of the land summoned our Rabbi to the palace. He was to come at once. When the Rabbi was standing before him, the Vizier, who was known to be both powerful and cruel, glared at him with terrible eyes and began to speak:

"I challenge you to a contest in sign language," he said in a loud, commanding voice. "Let one of your people come forward and I will speak to him with gestures and signs. You must find someone among you who can understand what I mean and can answer correctly in my sign language. If he fails, he loses the contest and also his life."

The Rabbi's heart pounded. His face turned pale. Who could meet such a challenge? What man or woman could understand the ruler's secret language?

"I give you thirty days to select someone and prepare him for this contest," continued the Vizier. "If nobody comes forward to accept my challenge, all of you will die, yes, everybody in the Jewish quarter." The Vizier drew himself up to his full height, held his head high, and smiled triumphantly.

Our brave Rabbi trembled with fear and anger. The wicked Vizier was obviously trying to rid Iraq of its Jews, starting with our community. Deeply troubled, the Rabbi went home. He sent word to all his people in the village to gather in the synagogue to pray and fast as they always did when threatened by the outside world.

Then he told them the Vizier's cruel scheme. He explained that one of them must accept the challenge to understand and to answer in a sign language only the Vizier knew.

"One of you must risk your life," he told them quietly. "Otherwise all of us will perish." Not a man among them thought he was wise enough to accept the Vizier's challenge.

One week passed, then two. Three weeks went by, and no one came forward. A steady hum of prayer came from the synagogue as the devout prayed for a miracle, so that their people would not be destroyed.

When the thirty days were almost up, Joseph the poultry dealer returned to the village from a long trip, bringing with him a great many chickens he had bought from the farms nearby. He went directly to the market to sell his fine poultry but was surprised to find that every shop was closed. Then he heard the murmur of voices in prayer coming from the synagogue.

"Oh," he worried, "have I forgotten? Is this the Sabbath or perhaps some other holy day?"

He hurried to the synagogue, where he found his wife, Sarah, praying with all the others.

"What on earth is the matter?" asked Joseph.

Sarah turned her frightened eyes toward him. "The cruel Vizier has demanded that one of us come forth to have a discussion with him in a sign language only he knows. If the volunteer fails to understand and to respond correctly, he will die. Worse still, if no one of our people meets the challenge, all of us will die. Isn't this enough to inspire us to pray for divine help?"

"Is that what all the wailing and praying is about?" exclaimed her husband in amazement. "Well, I'm ready to take up the challenge. Go to the Rabbi and say that I, Joseph the poultry dealer, will compete with the mighty Vizier."

"And what do you know about sign language, my husband? How will you understand him? You're only a poor poultry dealer!" exclaimed the good Sarah.

"What are you worried about? If no one volunteers, we all die. What do I lose by taking up the challenge? Perhaps this way I shall be able to save my people, my children, and you, my dear wife. For me, it is worth a try."

Sarah was frightened. Surely Joseph would fail in his brave attempt to save his people by engaging in a strange game of wits with the wicked Vizier, who wished them all dead. Deep inside her, however, Sarah admired and loved her husband for his courage and trusted his good sense. At last she agreed that he should take the risk. Together they went to find the Rabbi.

"O wise leader," said the poultry dealer, "let me be the one to compete with the cruel Vizier."

The Rabbi looked at Joseph for a long time. At last he spoke. "Bless you, my son," he murmured. "May God be with you both, Joseph and Sarah."

Finally the day of the contest arrived. Everyone gathered on the cobblestones of the village square. A man in a red cloak blew on a golden trumpet as the mighty Vizier entered the square. To the sound of martial music, he climbed up to his ornate seat, which had been raised on a high platform above the heads of the assembled crowd.

The Vizier looked down on all the people. When he saw that the lowly poultry dealer was the one who had taken up his challenge, he roared with laughter.

"Does this ignorant fellow really think he can understand my clever sign language?" he exclaimed, wiping tears of mirth from his eyes.

Then, turning to the poultry dealer, he asked condescendingly, "Joseph, do you understand what you must do?"

"I guess so," said Joseph in a voice so low that the people had to press forward to hear him.

"Remember, master of chickens," warned the Vizier, "you must watch the signs I make and you must understand exactly what they mean. Then you must answer me in the same way, with signs, so clearly that I understand your message."

"I know what I must do," replied Joseph in a whisper.

Everybody waited, tense, hardly breathing. The competition was about to begin.

The Vizier stood up and raised one finger. He held it high above his head and turned around so that everyone could see it. To the crowd he seemed to be saying:

"Poultry dealer, see one finger
Respond at once; don't dare linger."

Without hesitation, Joseph raised two fingers and showed them to the people, who imagined him responding:

"Why so much ado?
See my fingers, two."

The Vizier's face turned white. How had this ignorant fellow been able to understand him and respond so cleverly? The contest was not going as he had expected it to. He tossed his head and tried to smile, as if to say, "The first test was much too easy."

Then the Vizier took a slab of yellow cheese from his pocket. He held it up, smelled it, and let a look of pleasure come over his face, so that the people would know that the cheese was sweet and delicious. He seemed to be telling them:

"My second gesture is a tease.
I simply raise this piece of cheese."

Joseph the poultry dealer answered him at once by taking an egg from his own pocket and holding it up for all to see. He smiled as if he were thinking:

"Your second challenge is a breeze.
Here's my answer, if you please."

Although the Vizier was amazed at Joseph's response, he had no choice but to go on with the contest. He took a handful of grain from his pocket and, with a broad flourish, scattered the kernels on the ground. With that gesture, he appeared to boast:

"Seeds of grain I scatter wide;
Now look to heaven for your guide."

Joseph simply smiled, opened up his poultry coop, and set a hen free, as if he were announcing:

"Here's a hen to eat your seed.
How simple to match your every deed."

The hen wandered all about and gobbled up every one of the seeds. By this time, the Vizier was clearly astonished. When he had regained his composure, he called out in a loud voice to all the people:

"This man has matched my every sign!
He won the match. Now let us dine
On bread and cake and fish and wine
And dates and figs. This treat is mine."

The Rabbi and his people rejoiced to see the challenge end so happily, even though no one understood the Vizier's signs or Joseph's responses.

The Vizier's friends, disappointed at his defeat, gath-

ered around him. "What did your signs mean?" they asked
in puzzled voices. "The raised finger, the yellow cheese, the
scattered grain, what was all that about?" They pressed him
for explanations.

The Vizier held his hand up to stop the barrage of questions. Then he spoke slowly, sharing with his people what
happened during the contest:

"First, I raised one finger, meaning that there is only
one king. To my surprise, the poultry dealer raised two fingers, indicating that there are two kings, one in heaven and
one on earth. I was amazed at his wisdom.

"Next, I took out a piece of yellow cheese, meaning to
ask, 'Is this cheese from a white goat or a black one?' Now,
that was a very hard question, which I did not expect him
to answer correctly. But he took an egg from his pocket,
countering with his question, 'Is this egg from a white hen
or a brown?' Once more I marveled at the depth of his understanding.

"Finally, I scattered some grains of wheat on the ground,
meaning to taunt him because his people are scattered all
over the world. The poultry dealer answered me by freeing
his hen, who ate up all the grain. With this act he informed
me that the Messiah will come to gather the Jews from
wherever they are scattered on the face of the earth.

"Did you ever think a poultry dealer would be so clever?"

In the meantime, the Jews crowded around Joseph.
They all tried to speak at once. "How did you know what to
do? How did you understand his signs? How did you know
how to respond? What did it all mean?" they asked. Their
eyes were wide with wonder.

"It was simple," Joseph explained. "Did you see the
Vizier point at me with one finger, meaning to take out my
eye? Well, I pointed at him with two fingers, indicating, 'If
you do, I'll take out both your eyes.'

"Next, you remember, he held up a piece of cheese. He
meant to show that I was hungry and he was not. So I took
out an egg to let him know that I did not need his charity.

"Then he scattered some grains of wheat on the ground. I decided to feed my hen. She was hungry and I thought it would be a pity to waste all that grain."

The people around him smiled at Joseph and at each other, nodding their appreciation of his cleverness. Why had they not thought of that?

# Turkey

# 15

# SETTLING ACCOUNTS

In Turkey, we, too, told stories of Jews who succeeded in outwitting their tormentors. Let me tell you the tale of Eron the Turk, an itinerant peddler of glassware, who enjoyed taunting Zevulun, a Jewish shopkeeper and Eron's best customer.

It all happened in the ancient city of Istanbul, which some of you may still remember as Constantinople. The peddler Eron wandered throughout the city hawking, "Glasses for sale! Glassware for sale! Glass of all kinds for sale!"

Issachar, Eron's hardworking donkey, carried a heavy load of glassware on its back. The tired animal was relieved to hear its master's "Whoa!" which drew it to a halt in front of Zevulun's shop. There surely they would unload some of the weight chafing its back, for the Jewish shopkeeper had a flourishing trade in glassware.

Now, Eron the Turk, aware that Zevulun's younger brother had the same name as the donkey Issachar, delighted in taunting the Jewish shopkeeper. As Eron entered the shop, he would call out in a mocking voice, "Zevulun, your brother Issachar is out there, waiting for you!"

Grinning from ear to ear, the peddler Eron would gesture toward the ass laden with glassware standing patiently outside Zevulun's shop. The animal usually looked tired and dejected, head and ears pointing downward toward the earth.

You can imagine how painful this oft-repeated jibe was to Zevulun the shopkeeper, especially since his brother Issachar was a scholar, a very wise and respected man in Istanbul. Enraged, Zevulun would glare at Eron, but would say nothing. Inwardly, he would fume, "How am I going to punish this wretched peddler without losing my temper and my dignity?"

Eron, aware of the shopkeeper's frustration and anger, would then ask innocently, "What's the matter? Why are you so furious? You must know that your own Holy Scriptures refer to Issachar the bony ass!"

Now the Jew Zevulun was schooled in biblical studies. He knew of the Midrash, which told that the tribe of Zevulun became wealthy through sea trade and supported the tribe of Issachar, which devoted itself to the study of the Torah. He was proud that in his family, too, Issachar was the scholar and he the provider. He resented the disrespectful mockery directed at his beloved brother.

Zevulun's close Turkish neighbor, aware of all that was going on, would often ask his Jewish friend, "How come you remain silent? Why don't you punch that wretched peddler in the nose? Or at least tell him off?"

"I'm biding my time," Zevulun would respond. "Just you wait. You'll see me teach him a lesson in my own fashion."

On the morning of which I'm about to tell you, if you had gotten up really early, you would have seen Zevulun do some pretty strange things. First, he made his way stealthily to the public stables. He entered quietly and went from horse to horse, picking flies from ears, backs, legs, manes, and eyelids. When he had filled two fair-sized bags with these obnoxious creatures, he stuffed the bagfuls into his pockets, one on each side of his jacket.

He was cheerful and alert as he peered down the road, whistling a merry tune. Was he waiting for someone to arrive or perhaps for something to happen?

Soon in the distance, Issachar the ass appeared, the peddler at his side, both walking more slowly than usual.

The animal was heavily laden with glassware of all shapes, colors, and sizes. There were vases, bowls, trays, cups, saucers, and trivets, in clear white, green, blue, violet, yellow, persimmon, and even black glass.

"Whoa!" bellowed Eron the peddler. The grateful donkey stopped in front of Zevulun's shop.

In great humor, the peddler quipped his usual joke. "Zevulun, my friend, your brother Issachar is waiting outside to have a word with you." With a sly grin, he pointed to the exhausted donkey, who seemed to be snatching a nap.

"Yes, I know," responded Zevulun, apparently without anger. "I have to tell him some important family news. If you don't mind waiting a moment, I'll go outside and whisper it privately into my brother's ear."

The peddler was elated. "What fun!" he thought. "This idiot has swallowed my story hook, line, and sinker, and look at him, ready to talk into my donkey's ear!"

Aloud he replied, "Take your time, Zevulun. My business with you can wait . . . Talk with your brother as long as you wish. He's looked forward to seeing you this morning!"

Zevulun, hands in his pockets, casually strolled out to the donkey and leaned over its head as if to whisper into its ear. From his pockets, he took the two bags full of horseflies and emptied them quickly into the animal's long ears.

The unfortunate animal jumped up into the air as high as a champion show horse, heehawing in distress. The huge basket full of glassware tied to its saddle slid down its back. The glass crashed in a shower of multicolored fragments, splattering in every direction.

It was a sight to behold! Later, the Turkish neighbor entertained his friends with a detailed description of the incident. He was the only one who had actually witnessed the spectacular splash of colored glass as Zevulun took revenge for the years of humiliation and rage.

Of course, the peddler sued Zevulun. After all, wasn't

the shopkeeper responsible for the loss of Eron's property and income?

In court, Zevulun's defense was logical. "Your Honor, this peddler has for years visited me frequently in my shop and urged me to go out and talk with my brother Issachar, always pointing to his donkey who answers to that name.

"This time I had an important message for my brother. Our little sister, God willing, will be married next month. Since Issachar travels with the peddler every day, it is difficult to get a message to him. So I had to be the bearer of the good news. I told him the date of the wedding and urged him to be on time. I was not surprised when he started to dance for joy at our little sister's happiness and my parents' great hopes for her future."

The Judge could hardly suppress his smile. Turning to the peddler, he declared, "I am here to dispense justice. I understand that you yourself have repeatedly established the family relationship between Zevulun and your donkey. Is that true?"

"Yes, Your Honor, but . . ."

The Judge interrupted. "You did, by your own confession. Therefore, it follows that he was performing a familial duty by inviting his brother to their sister's wedding. You do agree to that, do you not?"

"Yes, Your Honor, but," put in the peddler, "I was only . . ."

The Judge continued. "Now you know what happens when a person makes a mockery of his fellowman. Perhaps you have learned a valuable lesson in this courtroom.

"This case is discharged without penalty, and Eron the peddler assumes total loss."

So the trial ended and they all went home.

The last I heard of this whole affair was that Eron the Turkish peddler bought a new stock of glassware, tied it on his donkey's back, and went hawking through the streets of Istanbul shouting, "Glasses for sale! Beautiful glassware for sale!"

When he arrived at Zevulun's shop, he shouted, "Whoa!" to his faithful donkey, who pulled up dutifully and waited half-asleep while its master sold beautiful glassware to Zevulun, the Jewish shopkeeper. Never again was there mention of the relationship between Issachar the donkey and Zevulun's brother, Issachar the scholar.

# Kurdistan

# 16

# THE KIND MIDWIFE

In Kurdistan, we preferred stories about fairies and other supernatural beings, even demons, which we called by the Hebrew name *shedim*.

I should explain at the outset that demons, or *shedim*, were not necessarily evil. There are stories about kind demons who performed deeds for the good of mankind.

For example, you may have read about Ashmodai, King of the Demons, who often protected ordinary people from impending harm. He also helped Solomon find the tiny worm Shamir, which cut the stones for the Temple in Jerusalem so that it could be built according to law without the use of metal.

My story is about demons who rewarded my grandmother, may she rest in peace, for her kindness to them. Indeed, my whole family benefited from her experience.

As a midwife, my grandmother—Sotte, we called her—helped women give birth to their babies. She never took money for her work because she enjoyed delivering infants. Furthermore, she was certain that she would receive her reward in the next world. Sotte was a very busy woman because there were no doctors in Zakho, our city, and she was the only midwife.

I have already mentioned that this story is about demons, or *shedim*, as we called them. So don't be surprised if I start by telling about a cat, a beautiful, sleek cat that crept into my grandmother's house one rainy night, so quietly that Sotte did not hear footsteps, because there were none.

Sotte was very tired, having delivered several babies that day. She had settled into her embroidery, which she found relaxing.

The shiny black cat, sniffing here and there, looked hungry. Grandma, tired as she was, stood up and set out a bowl of warm milk. And guess what! Sotte's practiced eye observed that the cat was pregnant!

Grandma's first thought was, "I would love to help this cat give birth. I want very much to be her midwife."

Now, this may seem a weird desire for Sotte to have had. Cats do not have midwives, do they? But be patient and hear me out.

One dark and stormy night a week later, my grandmother was wakened by a loud knock at her door. She was not frightened because she was used to people needing her in the middle of the night. She called out, "One moment! I'll get ready!"

She dressed in a hurry and opened the door without fear because, let me stress, midwives are often wakened in the middle of the night. Sotte was always ready to spring into action. On such a miserable night it would be like doing the 613 *mitzvot*, good deeds, all at once. It would be a shortcut to heaven!

On the threshold, wrapped in heavy rain gear, stood an agitated figure who spoke breathlessly. "Sotte, my wife is suffering terrible birth pains. Come quickly; there's no one else to help her. We'll pay you well for coming out in this terrible weather."

Now, Zakho is a small town and Sotte knew every inch of it. As she followed the strange figure up the main street, she couldn't help wondering why her footsteps were so loud and his not audible at all.

She soon noticed that they had left the houses behind. They were now walking in an open field beyond the town, where she knew nobody lived.

A strange feeling came over her. This figure must be a *shed*! What else? Her first instinct was to run away, to get back to the warmth and safety of her cozy home. Instantly, she knew that would be wrong. She realized for the first time that *shedim* must be helped in childbirth, and that was what she was good at.

"Please, God, be with me," she muttered under her breath. "I'm only doing a good deed, a *mitzvah*."

A long way from town, they reached a bridge made of stones seven meters square. Under the bridge to the left, they entered a huge cave. She heard a deep voice resounding with echoes. "Sotte, come in. You're just in time!"

My grandmother looked around. Of course, she knew about *shedim* and *shedot*, as male and female demons were called, and so do you, I'm sure. But who ever expects to see hundreds of them living together, singing and mewing like cats?

There were big ones, little ones, and middle-sized *shedim*. On their heads they all had horns, and even these were of different sizes and colors.

"Were you scared, Sotte?" we gasped in excitement when she told us the story.

She thought for a moment and replied, "Since you ask, no, by this time I was no longer frightened. I found the scene colorful and exciting. How many people have seen *shedim* at all, no less living together in a huge cave? I felt privileged. I may have looked scared, since I said nothing, not knowing what to say."

One *shed*, the one with the largest red horns, seemed to be the leader. He approached Grandma and said kindly but firmly, "We thank you for coming. But we must warn you: if the baby is a boy, you will get anything and everything you want. God forbid it should be a girl!"

Now, Grandma Sotte did get frightened. How could she determine the gender of a newborn infant? Such matters are in God's hands. She loved her grandchildren, boys and girls alike, and she could not understand why the *shedim* should prefer one to the other. But she said nothing.

Besides, she had work to do. A graceful young *shed* with purple horns took her by the hand, saying, "Sotte, follow me, please." He led her into a small bedroom.

Now, guess who was lying on the low bed? None other than the sleek and shiny cat that had visited her seven nights before! Sotte was about to get her wish to be midwife at this birth.

The cat in the pain of labor turned toward Sotte and whispered, "Thanks for coming, dear Sotte! I have not forgotten that you fed and cared for me last week, tired as you were. So listen to me carefully.

"Sotte, do not eat in this cave no matter how hungry, even when you are offered food. If you do, you will be transformed into a *shed* and you will never see your house, your children, or your grandchildren again."

My grandmother understood the cat's warning. She determined that she would accept no refreshment served by the *shedim*. Although she remained in the demons' cave all night and was offered tempting, delicious food and drink, she neither ate nor drank. In order to avoid hurting her hosts' feelings, she told them that she was respecting a Jewish fast day honoring the dead.

With her sleeves rolled up, she cared for the cat tenderly. In the morning, a male kitten was born.

What rejoicing there was in the cave! The *shedim* laughed, danced, and sang until the cave rang with the sound of music and joyous celebration.

The chief of the demons, the one with the longest red horns, approached my grandmother and thanked her. "Sotte," he said, "ask for whatever your heart desires. We are grateful to you, and we want to make sure that you are fully rewarded for your expert care and the infant's safe birth. Ask for whatever you want or need."

"I don't want or need anything," responded Grandma. "I am happy to have done a good deed and feel that I have already been rewarded by the opportunity you gave me to do it."

"You must take something," he urged. "It is our custom to give generous rewards, and you must not disregard our customs."

A sharp tone in his voice made Sotte aware that she must not treat this situation lightly. She would have to respect the ways of the *shedim.*

Luckily, through the corner of her eye she glimpsed a heap of garlic lying in a dark corner of the cave. She really needed garlic for her cooking, she remembered.

"Since you are so kind, please let me have some of your fresh garlic. I would appreciate that very much," she said quietly.

The demons gathered together as much garlic as they could stuff into her deep pockets. Then they escorted Grandma, tired and happy, to her home in Zakho.

Sotte was exhausted from the long walk to and from the demons' cave and from delivering the infant, without food or drink all night long. She let herself into her house, locked the door behind her, threw the bunches of garlic in a heap on the floor, and sank into her bed.

The next thing she knew, the sun was streaming into her room and I was standing over her asking, "Where did you get all that gold, Sotte?"

"What are you talking about, child? I took no gold. You know I'm not paid for my work because I do it for love and enjoyment. Besides, why do you wake me so early?" Grandma rubbed her eyes sleepily.

"Look, Sotte!" I shouted in great excitement. "Look at all the gold in the corner against the door!"

Sure enough, the garlic flung down the night before had been transformed into pure gold.

Dear Sotte didn't want any of it for herself. She was determined to refuse any kind of reward for her work. Besides, I think that she still harbored some fear that if she accepted anything from the *shedim*, there would be danger of her being transformed into one of them. And she did love being a grandma!

How did Sotte solve the problem of the gold? She gave equal amounts of it to all her grandchildren.

We have all grown old now and have children and grandchildren of our own. Our family is scattered, some in the United States, some in Canada, and even some in Australia.

My sister and I made *aliyah* to Israel, where we are very happy. Each of us still has a piece of the golden garlic, which we have mounted on a stick and keep as a memento of our loving Sotte, the midwife who was rewarded by *shedim* against her wish. The golden garlic has always brought us good luck and, God willing, always will.

# Libya

# 17

# THE DEVIL OUTWITTED

Let's stay with the supernatural a while longer. In my country, Libya, *shedim*, or demons, and even the devil himself enter into our folktales quite naturally. It's as if it were a commonplace experience to encounter supernatural beings on the street, in homes, just anywhere.

In one of our stories, the devil engages in a life-and-death struggle with an ordinary young boy. I think you'll like the way it turns out.

Once not so long ago, a mother and her teenage son, David, lived together in a Libyan village where it was not easy for a widow to eke out a living. She looked forward to the time when the young boy would be mature enough to help her.

David, however, was so wrapped up in his own dreams that he seemed unable to concentrate and do things right. He had all kinds of weird ideas and even invented some pretty clever contraptions.

It was fine to be imaginative and inventive, but these were not the talents that would help his mother keep her family in clothes, her fireplace burning, and her table with food on it. Since she faced these tasks all by herself, she tried to persuade her son to learn something practical, a trade of some sort.

I'm not implying that the boy didn't try. First, he took a job with the blacksmith, who sympathized with the plight of the poor family and hired David as his helper. You'll find it hard to believe, but on the very first day of work, David missed the anvil. His hammer hit the blacksmith's hand instead. The smithy, howling with pain, sent him for the doctor. As you can imagine, the unfortunate blacksmith threw David out of the shop and told him never to return.

Next, the village cobbler, hearing of the disaster in the forge, pitied the boy and his mother, and offered to teach David the very useful trade of repairing and even making shoes. Again, it will be hard to believe what happened! In the first half hour, David pushed an awl through the leather of a new pair of shoes and pierced the cobbler's right arm. Frightened, the unhappy boy ran away.

Running as fast as his legs would carry him, David fled to the edge of the village where meadows and hills stretched ahead of him. Still he kept on running, even though he had never been so far away from home. By now nothing looked familiar to him.

Breathless, he slowed down to a walk and suddenly found himself in front of a magnificent castle that he had never heard of or seen. He entered the courtyard and became fascinated by the beautiful gardens where flowers, blooming bushes, and blossoming trees grew in many-colored profusion.

Finally, he came to a stone wall separating the courtyard and gardens from the open country behind the palace. He climbed up. Stretching on all sides as far as he could see were seemingly endless fields of lush grass, where sheep and goats grazed by the side of a huge herd of cattle. He looked around to find the shepherd.

I'm not sure that I should tell you now, because certainly David did not find out so quickly, but the person who tended these animals was none other than the devil himself. He smiled at David and asked what had brought him to these grazing grounds. After hearing the lad's story, the devil invited him into the palace.

In the days and weeks that followed, the devil learned to appreciate the boy's originality and ingenuity. He became so fond of David that he taught him diabolical sorcery and magic. David became an apt learner and soon gained confidence in his ability to do things well. The witchcraft he excelled in was the art of changing from one form to another.

As time went by, the devil began to trust David. It came to pass that one day, about to leave for a short trip, the devil handed David the keys to the palace.

Patting the boy fondly on the shoulder, he said, "I want you to feel at home in my palace. You may use these keys to enter all the rooms except the large attic. If you remember that, all will go well with you during my absence." A moment later he was gone.

By now you know David well enough to expect that he would climb up to the attic immediately and would open the door. What do you think he saw in the forbidden room?

What he saw was so gruesome and so appalling that I don't feel it would be right to describe it to all of you, since there are many young people in this audience. Suffice it to say that his blood turned cold and he stood transfixed, gazing at the horrible sight before him.

When he came to, he realized what his fate would be if he remained in the palace. It was clear that the devil was somewhat like Bluebeard, who murdered many victims. He evidently delighted in teaching magic arts and sorcery to young men and then doing away with them before they could use this demonic knowledge.

Obviously, David, who had run away from the blacksmith and the cobbler out of fear, escaped from the palace as fast as he could. Since a horse was the fastest animal he could think of, he used his knowledge of sorcery to transform himself into a graceful black racing steed.

He galloped back to town. Seeing the Governor's stables full of horses, many of them black, he joined the herd. He was certain that he would remain hidden in the pack, and that eventually he would escape.

This was not to be! That very day the devil, already on his trail, recognized David and immediately transformed himself into a dappled gray mare, which stood next to the black steed in the royal stable.

Aware of the danger, David immediately used his magical powers to become a house standing in a row of similar houses on a street in a row of similar streets. This transformation would surely protect him, he thought.

Not so. The devil immediately joined him as an adjacent house. David made his house crumble as if bombed. As he was fast becoming a pile of rubble, he changed himself into a strong pack-camel and joined a caravan in a far-off desert. This disguise would be impenetrable, he was certain.

Not so. Immediately, a strange Bedouin, head swathed in *kaffiyeh* and *agol*, bought him. This proved to be the disguise of the devil, who drove him together with many other camels across the desert sands to the seaside.

Forced into the sea, he would have drowned had he not plunged into the foaming waves as a fish with glistening scales. The devil leaped in after him as a hungry shark.

Before the devil had submerged, however, David was soaring up to heaven as a glorious eagle, head high, enjoying his freedom in the blue skies above the clouds. Into the firmament flew another eagle in hot pursuit, the devil himself.

David swooped down to the royal palace and flew into the window of the royal Princess's room. There he became a ring of diamonds, rubies, and emeralds, hidden among the fabulous jewels locked in the box in which the King's daughter kept her favorite jewelry. Surely he would be safe now and would be able to rest from his strenuous effort to rid himself of the pursuing devil.

Not so. In a few moments, the devil joined him as a bracelet of diamonds, rubies, and emeralds, an exact match to his ring. Immediately David became a soft luscious peach resting among the colorful fruits in a blue glass fruit bowl on the King's dining table.

Before the devil could reach for it, the peach was transformed into a grape hidden among other grapes in a cluster of red muscats. The devil attempted to grasp the bunch in which David was hidden.

The boy, however, had already become a large red-ripe pomegranate containing hundreds of glistening seeds, all alike, hardly distinguishable. As the devil grabbed at the round pomegranate, David thought he had surely lost his flight for freedom. But the slippery fruit fell to the ground and splattered, the seeds scattering in every direction.

The wily devil quickly changed into a rooster, which ate the seeds, swallowing them whole with such speed that they were all gone in a second, except for one. David had to think fast if he wanted to survive, for that one seed was all that was left of him.

He quickly transformed that one seed into a sharp knife, which in one fell blow slaughtered the rooster. The devil was dead!

The knife changed into a young man, who resembled David but was older and had gained maturity from the experiences that I have told you about. He was handsome and dashing and was ready for more adventures,which he hoped would be of a different sort. I don't see how he could stand any more of what he had just gone through. Do you? I'll tell you more about him and his adventures next year at our storytelling festival.

# Germany

# 18

# ISHTAR,
# THE MORNING STAR

Have you ever gotten up early enough to see the morning star shining in the east when the dawn starts coloring the sky? Have you wondered how this lovely star came to compete with the sun as it chases away the darkness of the night?

Now that it's my turn, I'd like to tell you how we in Germany have been explaining the presence of the morning star, brightest of all stars in the firmament, before the night is entirely conquered by the sun. This story is full of magic, of angels, of sorcerers, of heaven and earth; even God takes part in it.

It all started a long, long time ago before Noah and the great flood. Indeed, this story explains why the world was flooded, as well as how the morning star took its important place in the dawning sky.

A long time ago, as I said, before the flood, the angels, Shemhazai and Azael, looked down on earth and saw how bad people had become. The two of them were so distressed that they dared to appear before the Lord, saying, "Dear Lord, there must be an end to the wicked ways of the world. Wrongdoers must be punished, or evil will triumph over good. Then you will have no choice but to destroy all mankind and create a new world."

In his wisdom, the Holy One pointed out that if they were on earth they, too, would behave in the evil ways of men and women. He did, however, finally agree to allow the two angels to descend to earth as tall, good-looking men. Shemhazai and Azael hoped to persuade people to live in peace and harmony, to be kind to each other and honest in their dealings.

Before they departed for their sojourn on earth, Shemhazai and Azael made two promises to God. The first was never to reveal the secrets of Heaven. It was clear that nothing and nobody could make them break that vow. They also agreed that they would never marry a human. This last vow, as you may imagine, caused a great deal of trouble.

They arrived in a country whose King had two very beautiful daughters, Ishtar and Naamah. As the two angels entered the palace, handsome and splendidly dressed, angel Shemhazai and princess Ishtar were immediately attracted to each other, as were Azael and Naamah.

The two angels knew a great many feats of sorcery. They offered to amuse the king and his courtiers by performing some of their magic.

Shemhazai went first. He gazed deeply into Ishtar's eyes and bowed gracefully to the men and women of the court. Then he quickly changed himself into an eagle, flew out the window, and a moment later flew back with a magnificent rose in his beak. Alighting on Ishtar's arm, he dropped the flower in her lap and changed back to his handsome human form. He bowed, smiled at Ishtar, and took his seat.

Now it was Azael's turn. As all eyes focused on him, the walls of the palace disappeared. A sea of water roared in around the courtiers, waves dashing against their chairs, white foam splattering even the thrones of the King and his Queen.

Everybody screamed in terror. With a smile at Naamah, Azael gestured toward the raging sea, and the water subsided. The whole court wondered that he had been able to create a mirage that had deceived them all.

As the applause thundered through the court, the two sorcerers approached the princesses. Shemhazai stood before Ishtar, Azael before Naamah. Both took off their hats and with broad flourishes, bowed low before the princesses. To everyone's amazement, a cascade of sweet-scented white gardenias fell in profusion from their hats and covered the feet of the delighted young women.

The King realized immediately that with these two men at his side he could rule the world. Why, they could make anything happen. And his daughters seemed to enjoy their company well enough. He decided then and there that his daughters would be the brides of these very attractive and gifted sorcerers.

I am sure you can guess what happened next. The two angels, who had fallen in love with the two princesses, forgot their solemn promise to the Holy One. A date was set for the two royal weddings.

That night, Ishtar had a disturbing dream that put an end to these happy plans. Old Enoch, God's messenger, appeared before her while she slept, and revealed that the two sorcerers were in reality angels sent down to earth as messengers of God.

Enoch told her of their promise to God not to marry while on earth. If they were to break this solemn oath, their offspring would be *Nephillim*, cruel and terrible giants who would poison the world with evil. The Holy One would have no alternative but to destroy all life on earth and start the creative process all over again.

Horrified and deeply frightened, Ishtar looked up at the old man with tears in her eyes. "I understand that I must not marry my beloved Shemhazai. I could not tolerate bearing children who would grow into wicked giant *Nephillim*. Our love would then have caused the end of the world as we know it."

Ishtar awoke. The moon was still high in the sky. She lay in bed, horrified at the thought that the fate of all the people on earth depended on two sisters' giving up the men they loved.

She knew what she must do. She would tell Naamah

what she had learned, and together they would agree to sacrifice their own personal happiness.

In the cold moonlight, Ishtar woke Naamah and told her the message delivered by Enoch, the messenger of God. To Ishtar's amazement, her sister would not believe any part of the warning revealed by Enoch in the dream. Naamah totally rejected the notion that the two brilliant sorcerers were angels bound in oath to the Lord not to marry, lest their offspring be evil giant *Nephillim* who would bring about the end of the world.

"Are you saying that my marriage must not take place because of this weird story told in a dream?" she exclaimed. She absolutely refused to give up her beloved Azael.

What should Ishtar do? In her distress, she went back to sleep. Again Enoch, the messenger of God, appeared before her. He was aware of Naamah's stubborn refusal, and consoled Ishtar.

"You alone can save the people on this earth," he told her. If one sister resists marrying her angel, the punishment inflicted will be lessened. Because of your sacrifice, one man, his wife, and his family will be spared, as well as a pair of every kind of animal and bird. From these remnants, the world will be renewed."

Ishtar knew now that she on her own could save the earth from total destruction. Painful though it was, she told Shemhazai that she knew he was an angel under oath to God.

"We must part," she sobbed, "sad as our separation will make us both."

Shemhazai realized immediately how wicked his behavior had been, that he actually had reneged on a solemn promise to God. He embraced Ishtar for the last time murmuring, "Good-bye, my beloved."

In Heaven there was rejoicing and great admiration for Ishtar, a woman who cared more for the future of the world than for her own happiness. As a reward, she was placed in the sky as the morning star, which competes in brightness with the sun itself.

You wonder about Naamah. Yes, she married Azael. Their children were the dreadful *Nephillim*, huge giants who brought evil to the world. So widespread was the wickedness that the Holy One had no choice but to cause a great flood to cover the lands, killing people, animals, and vegetation.

Because of Ishtar's unselfish decision to give up her own happiness, Noah and his family survived the flood together with pairs of all animals then on earth. Thus there was a bridge to the human beings of today, who still have a chance to create a better world. Hopefully, there will no longer be a reason to destroy us all and start anew.

Now you know why the morning star is so gloriously positioned in the sky and why we all admire its beauty when we get up early enough to see it. If it were not for Ishtar, we would not be here to gaze up at all.

# The Netherlands

# 19

## AZAEL VERSUS KING SOLOMON

I loved your story about Ishtar and Shemhazai and how Ishtar was placed in the dawning sky as the beautiful morning star. It reminds me of a story we have told in the Netherlands for hundreds of years about Azael and his evil behavior. Let me tell it to you now, because it is a natural sequel to the story about Ishtar's sacrifice.

Evidently the fallen angel Azael never repented having broken his promise by marrying Naamah. He also did not regret that he and Naamah had peopled the earth with evildoers who had to be destroyed by the flood. He himself continued to inflict so much cruelty and suffering that the cries of the people reached Heaven.

Again, God intervened. He sent the angel Raphael to earth to punish Azael.

Now, Raphael had been given great power by God so that he could overwhelm Azael and put him in chains. Once that was done, Raphael transported the helpless Azael to a barren desert called Dudael, where he hung the fallen angel upside down in a rocky canyon. There, among the sharp and rugged promontories, Azael was to remain without human contact, suspended in darkness.

But Azael's wicked imagination was still active. He realized that he still had the ability to send out messages from his uncomfortable perch in the craggy desert. With his

magic powers, he contacted all the evil beings in those dark
mountains, giving them a sense of his whereabouts.

Soon he was no longer alone. All the fiery serpents,
demons, and evil spirits were drawn to him. They surrounded him in the desert, eager to learn the dark secrets
of magic and demonology known only to the fallen angel
Azael.

Among the evil beings who heard Azael's siren call was
a wicked magician, Merdel, a man who for many years had
been deeply involved with the dark secrets of the demonic
underworld. He knew that Azael still had formidable knowledge about evil even though he was suspended upside down
in the canyon of sharp boulders above the bleak and craggy
desert.

Merdel the magician, whose reputation was so awful his
name was rarely mentioned, was delighted to join the demons and evil spirits as they swarmed toward the fallen
angel. Azael, in turn, welcomed this man whose evil exploits
were well known in the nether world.

The fallen angel decided that he would use wicked
Merdel to inflict evil on the world. Dangling in the dark
cavern, Azael himself was helpless. He would therefore have
to teach the magician everything he knew.

For forty days Merdel remained with Azael, the fallen
angel, learning all the dark secrets of wizardry and magic
that had never before been known by any earthly being. He
eagerly soaked up this forbidden knowledge. He remembered every detail of Azael's demonology. When he left the
dark canyon, he was conducted by serpents and demons
away from the craggy desert of Dudael to areas inhabited
by people. He was intent on controlling and ruling the world
in ways the evil angel Azael had taught him.

This he did. Wherever he went he left a trail of wickedness and suffering behind him. Bad deeds were rewarded
and kind acts were punished. Soon the evil effects of the
magician's deeds became so widespread that King Solomon
heard of his great and awesome power.

You know how wise King Solomon was. What you may not know is that he was also famed for his good deeds. Although he knew a great deal about sorcery, his knowledge came from the Holy One and he used it only for the benefit of people.

How could he use his own great magical power to defeat the wicked magician whom Azael had succeeded in making the most dangerous man in the world? King Solomon was determined to get rid of the evil sorcerer and the influence of Azael at the same time.

What complicated matters was that the magician, through his own powerful trickery, was already aware of the King's intention. He vowed to challenge and overcome King Solomon.

Soon the most dangerous villain in the world was pitted against the wisest human being, who was intent on eradicating evil. The conflict involved the forces of Light and of Darkness in a struggle for the future of mankind. Who would be victorious in this awesome encounter?

Now, it was common knowledge that King Solomon always wore a signet ring with four precious stones. The wicked sorcerer had learned through his contact with the nether world that this was no ordinary piece of jewelry. He knew that all of the King's superhuman talents were derived from this ring, a gift of four powerful angels, each of whom had engraved a letter of God's name on one of the four jewels. All of King Solomon's magical powers came from this ring. Without it he could perform no sorcery at all.

Merdel, the wicked magician, determined to steal the King's ring. If he could accomplish this theft, he would be the most powerful person on earth and Solomon would be powerless. How he would do this was the question.

The King wore the ring all day and all night. He never removed it, nor would it be possible to steal it from his finger. A plan had to be devised to induce him to slip off the powerful magic keepsake. It would be smooth sailing after that.

The diabolical Merdel finally came up with a clever scheme. He recalled the story of Solomon's attraction to the Queen of Sheba and realized that the great King had one big weakness: beautiful women who were also wise.

Now, you must have heard of Lilith, the incredibly beautiful woman who, according to legend, had been married to Adam, the first man. She had lost her place in the Garden of Eden by speaking the forbidden name of God. She had then flown to the nether world of demons, serpents, and witches, where she lived in a cave near the sea. From time to time, always at night, she would fly out to perform some particularly evil form of witchcraft known only to the most astute necromancers in the dark underworld.

Lilith was as unscrupulously wicked as she was enchantingly lovely and intelligent, the perfect choice for the magician's plan to defeat King Solomon. She would catch him off guard to get possession of his ring, and with it gain unlimited power for the fallen angel Azael and the wicked magician Merdel, as well as for herself. Together, the three evil tricksters would rule the world mercilessly.

Unaware of this nefarious plot, Solomon was doing what he usually did at night. He was reading the Torah. Suddenly, the letters started to move in concentric circles, jumping off the page when they came to the edge. Soon, all the pages of his precious Book were entirely blank. What could have caused this terrible destruction? Surely, there must be some deep meaning, perhaps a warning of evil in his room.

Just then, he felt the soft touch of a hand on his. When he looked up, a young woman stood close by, alluring him with her stunning beauty. She was about to put her arms around his neck and her cheek on his. He was about to fall under her spell.

He suddenly thought, "How did this woman gain access to my private quarters? How did she slither past the guards? How did she slip into my locked bedroom? Why did the letters disappear from the pages of my Torah? This woman must be the source of the evil I feel pervading my presence."

King Solomon took the lovely lady's hand and, pretending to like her, led her to a large mirror. She looked up. To her surprise, she did not see her beautiful face reflected there. Something was wrong.

Lilith quickly understood that Solomon had caught on to her trickery. She promptly used her witchcraft to vanish from his presence and indeed from the world of humanity. She returned to the dark caverns of the demonic underground from which the magician had summoned her to do his evil bidding. She is probably still there, hoping to be called upon again to inflict evil on human beings during her forages into the night.

Lilith's defeat by King Solomon proved a total disaster to the forces of evil unleashed by Azael. The fallen angel himself is still hanging upside down in the dark and forsaken desert of Dudael among the sharp, pointed stones of the canyon where he was placed by Raphael.

I'm sure you will agree that this was an appropriate punishment for an angel who had broken a solemn promise to God. Remember that he and the princess Naamah had peopled the world with evil giant *Nephillim* who had to be destroyed by the great flood. Only the family of Noah and the animals on the ark were saved to renew life on the earth. This was the gift of Ishtar.

As for the magician Merdel, who had conspired with Azael and Lilith, he received his just punishment for the great suffering he had inflicted on mankind and for his plot against Solomon and the forces of Light. He was forced out of the world of humanity into which he was born. His wicked soul joined Lilith in the dark world of demons. There it flies, perpetually making circles above her cave by the sea, where she is entrapped until evil is again unleashed. Hopefully, that will never happen.

# Poland

# 20

# GETZEL THE PHILOSOPHER

**W**hile some of you were telling fantastic tales about demons and devils, magic and sorcery, I thought about the gentle stories we tell in Poland about the foolish people of Chelm. Not that we believe the Chelmites are really fools. I've been to Chelm many times, and the people there are ordinary folk like you and me. Chelm has its share of wise people as well as of fools, and all shades in-between.

But somehow, folklore has dubbed them foolish, and they are good enough sports and have a good enough collective sense of humor to go along with the legendary myth of their foolishness. Besides, the tales told about them, although fictional, are very funny. And they laugh as we do at the silly situations in these stories.

There are many stories about Chelm and you must have heard some of them. I would like to tell you one you may not have heard.

A long time ago, Getzel became known as the philosopher of Chelm. You may wonder how this happened. It all came about quite logically.

Before Getzel was called a philosopher, he was just an ordinary man who came home from work and sat on a chair to rest until his wife gave him a cup of tea and a *kichel*. (For your information, this is a very light cookie weighing almost nothing.) At this point, he would become very talkative, pick up a child, kiss a little, drink a little, and eat a little, like most husbands.

This particular day I'm telling you about, he came home and just kept sitting in the same position. Even when the tea was served, he didn't move to take the glass in his hand, he didn't drink or eat, and what's even worse, he didn't talk at all, not to his wife, nor to his children.

"Getzel, what are you doing?" asked his wife.

"Thinking," answered Getzel.

"What are you thinking about?" his wife cried out, alarmed because he had never claimed to be doing that before.

"How can I answer such a foolish question?" quipped Getzel. "The thought is still hatching in my head. Just leave me alone while I think!"

To make a long story short, Getzel sat at the diningroom table, his head cupped in his hand, neither eating nor drinking, neither talking nor moving, just thinking for three days and three nights. All this time, his wife pleaded with him to at least eat something, to take a drink. Now she began to worry for his life. After all, he might starve to death and leave her a widow from all this nonsense.

When things became this serious in Chelm, the Rabbi was called in, of course. And this time was no exception.

The Rabbi came with a group of respected citizens, whom he picked up along the way, to help him judge the seriousness of Getzel's condition as reported by his wife. Sure enough, they found Getzel sitting at the dining-room table, staring ahead with a blank, glazed look, apparently just simply thinking.

The Rabbi was impressed and said kindly, "Getzel, tell us what your thoughts are about so far, and we'll try to help you resolve the problem you are considering. You can't go on like this. You haven't eaten in days, and you look pale and drawn. Nobody can think for such a long time and live. You are probably sick already."

Getzel begged for another day of thinking, and the

Rabbi, respectful of thinkers, granted his request. The next morning, after four days and four nights of sleeplessness and starvation, Getzel pleaded for still more time to finish his thinking.

This was just too much for the Rabbi to countenance. He said sternly, "Getzel, you must stop thinking and have something to eat. You are endangering your health, indeed your very existence. That is a grievous sin, for human life is more important than anything else in this world, even thinking. You must break your fast."

When the Rabbi commanded in that tone of voice, everybody knew that he meant it. The best thing to do—if his connections with the next world were to be of any benefit at all—would be to obey him. Getzel did just that.

He stopped thinking and sat down to a good meal that had been waiting for him. The Rabbi and his coterie of Chelmites waited respectfully for Getzel to finish eating to the last lick of his fingers.

By now, their curiosity was overwhelming. They all leaned forward to listen when the Rabbi finally said, "Now, Getzel, take a little drink of wine to wash it all down and tell us what on earth all that thinking was about."

Getzel was upset. "You made me stop thinking in the middle of my thoughts. I never did come to any conclusions. How am I supposed to tell you what it was all about if I don't know myself?"

The Rabbi was getting short of patience as well. "Getzel," he responded as calmly as he could, "you have thought for four days and four nights. Surely you have something you can tell us about these thoughts!"

"Well," said Getzel, "if I must share with you before I have completed my thinking process, I'll tell you what I came up with in the four days and nights.

"A profound idea entered my head and I pursued it as far as I could in the short time you gave me. I imagined all the men in the world coming together to make one gigantic man. Then I visualized all the trees in all of the forests coming together to make one huge tree. And then I went further and envisioned all the rivers becoming one enormous river. Soon I imagined all the axes on the earth combining to become an immense ax . . ."

The Chelmites, in their desire to hear the conclusion of Getzel's thought, by this time were leaning so far forward that they almost toppled over onto Getzel and the Rabbi. "And what did you think would happen next?" they asked with bated breath.

"Then I thought, if this gigantic man were to raise the immense ax and chop down the huge tree, do you have any idea—just try to imagine—"

The Chelmites could hardly contain their impatience and curiosity. "What are you saying? Don't stop! Go on!" urged the men of Chelm.

"Imagine if this huge tree with its tremendous branches covered by millions of leaves were to fall into this enormous river, how high do you think the splash would be? That was what I was thinking of when you interrupted me and made me eat instead of think.

"I was about to determine whether the splash would rise up as far as Heaven, or perhaps even higher. And now all those hours of thinking have been wasted. I can no longer pick up the thread of my thoughts, and I shall never know the answer to this important question."

Getzel looked very unhappy until one of the Chelmites exclaimed, full of admiration, "Only a brilliant mind could have had these deep thoughts and posed this great question. Getzel is truly a great thinker, a logician, a philosopher!"

"We should make him our official philosopher," suggested another of the wise men of Chelm, stroking his beard and twirling his side curls. He, too, was thinking deeply as he made this brilliant suggestion, which caught on.

After the incident of which I have told you, Getzel was known as the philosopher of Chelm. Indeed, since then, he has been given all the honor and respect due to a person who had earned this prestigious title fairly and brilliantly.

# Hungary

# 21

# THE POWER OF SHOES

In my *shtetl*, too, we used to tell tales about the foolish Chelmites. Now that you have heard the story of how Getzel became known as the official philosopher of Chelm, you surely must realize there's more to be told about that. The great thinker was bound to have amusing experiences simply because of the title he had earned and the fame that came with it. I'd like to tell you one of his adventures that resulted from the respect in which he was held as "philosopher."

One day, after a great fire had ruined a wedding feast and destroyed a good part of the town, the elders of Chelm assembled in their meetinghouse. I won't tell you about the fire because that's too long a story. We'll leave that for another time. Suffice it to say that the Chelmites were determined never again to allow a fire to get so destructive.

But how could they prevent a fire from spreading after it got started? They had heard that in Warsaw, fires don't burn down so much of the city because the people are very smart about things like that. They have had so much experience that they know what to do. After much discussion and many serious suggestions, the elders decided to send someone to Warsaw to find out how to put out fires.

But who should go to Warsaw? They thought long and carefully, smoothing down their bearded chins to sharpen their minds. The upshot of it all was that they chose Getzel the philosopher by unanimous vote. The title assured them that he was the right man for the job.

Getzel was delighted. He had always been restless and had dreamed of seeing the world. He was particularly excited about visiting Warsaw, because a merchant passing through the town had described the wonders of the capital vividly. What an opportunity to travel!

The morning of the trip to Warsaw, Getzel awoke at dawn, wound his *tefillin*, or phylacteries, around his arms and head, said his morning prayers as usual, and added a special request for a safe and successful journey. He packed some bread and hard-boiled eggs into his knapsack, which he slung over his shoulder, and took his walking stick from its place against the wall. He kissed the *mezuzah* as he went out the door and started walking toward Warsaw, singing aloud joyously at the thought of seeing the city at last.

It was still very early, yet he could feel the heat of the day and the dust of the road rising into his nostrils. After he had trudged along for several hours, the sun rose high in the sky and he began to feel pangs of hunger.

Just then, it seemed to him that a green oasis appeared in the distance. He pushed on and sure enough, he came to a grove of trees and found a spring of fresh water nearby.

"The Lord is watching over me today," he thought, as he settled down for a short rest in the shade of a tree. He ate his noonday meal of bread and eggs, and took a long drink of cool water.

Since he was tired and dusty, he decided to take a little snooze. The philosopher in him figured, "What would be the harm in that?"

As usual, he continued ruminating. "I'm facing a real problem here. If I fall asleep, I'll be unconscious for a while. Who knows how long? The problem is: how can I be sure that when I get up, I'll remember the direction to Warsaw?"

At this point, he realized he was not called the philosopher of Chelm for nothing. He was always full of ideas, and this time was no exception. "I know the solution to this dilemma," he thought, and swung into action.

"What did he do?" you're wondering.

It was a simple idea, and took no time at all to accomplish. He removed his shoes from his tired feet and put them on the road in front of him, toes pointing toward the capital city and away from Chelm. Now he could fall asleep under a tree in a relaxed frame of mind, because when he awoke to resume his journey, his shoes would tell him the direction to Warsaw.

He immediately fell into a sound sleep.

In that quiet part of Poland, not many people were on the road between Chelm and Warsaw at noon in the heat of the day. One farmworker did happen to pass by, however. He saw what to him was a very funny sight, a pair of very dusty well-worn shoes stuck out in the middle of the road.

He picked them up, looked at them critically with an eye to taking them with him, but finally decided they had too many holes to make it worthwhile. He dropped them, and as they fell, they turned around so they faced in the other direction. Humming cheerfully, he continued on his way and forgot the whole incident.

When Getzel awoke after a refreshing nap, he looked at his shoes, carefully noting the position of the toes. He took another cool drink at the spring and splashed some of the soothing water on his face and hands. Only then did he put on his shoes, happy and confident in the knowledge that they were pointing the way to Warsaw.

After walking in that direction for several hours, Getzel saw the roofs of a city in the distance. Before long he reached a cemetery, which, he figured out, must be on the outskirts of all towns. Even so, he wondered at how much this scene of a village burial ground resembled that of Chelm, which he had left behind him early that morning.

He thought philosophically, "This is my first trip out of Chelm, and I see that the good Lord was evenhanded and made all cities and towns alike so there would be equality among the peoples on this earth."

Nevertheless, he couldn't help wondering how much the capital city, which he had heard so much about, looked like his beloved *shtetl*, the Chelm he knew so well. There was the town hall with horses and wagons hitched to white posts. Then came the marketplace, which had the same stalls for fish, vegetables, and secondhand clothing, lined up in the same order. Even the vendors resembled those he knew back home.

As he strolled on, he passed the synagogue. To his amazement, the building was an exact replica of the one he prayed in every Sabbath and weekday mornings and evenings. He peeked in, and was astonished to see that the cantor and rabbi of the Warsaw synagogue looked remarkably like his own revered leaders in Chelm. Getzel was delighted.

What surprised him most of all was the street just behind the bathhouse, which looked exactly like the street he lived on. He pondered, "I wonder if the people who live here suffer from the heat escaping from the steam room in the summer and benefit from its warmth in the winter time, the way we do."

"Will wonders never cease?" he murmured, stroking his beard thoughtfully. Since he was a philosopher, he added, "I guess there is nothing new in this universe. I suppose cities, towns, and villages throughout the world must all look alike!" He strolled on past the bathhouse.

"I wonder if on this street that is just like mine, there is a house like mine," he mused.

Getzel walked up the street, which had a slight incline, making him breathe heavily as he always did when returning home. He stopped short in total astonishment in front of a house precisely like his own. He stood there twirling his sideburns and staring in disbelief.

From inside the house he heard a woman chiding in a voice just like that of his wife, Malka, "Children, stop running around. Your noisemaking is giving me a headache! Won't you help me a bit while your father is away? I can't do everything by myself!"

"In a minute, Mama! I'm busy!"

The child's voice sounded like his son's. Could there be two Bereles, one in Warsaw and one in Chelm, always saying, "I'll help you later"?

He stood there, hesitating to intrude on this strange woman and her children. Then she stepped out of the doorway onto the porch, the spitting image of Malka!

When she saw him, she cried out, "Getzel! What are you doing here? Am I glad you're home already! Maybe the children will do as I say now that their father is back. But how come you returned so soon?"

Without waiting for a reply, this strange woman calmed down a bit, and continued, "As long as you're here just in time for evening prayers, go to the synagogue, Getzel. All your cronies are waiting to hear what you learned today on your journey. I am curious, too, but you'll tell me when you come home."

Getzel was flabbergasted. Could there be two Malkas just alike, one in Chelm and one in Warsaw? Bewildered, he turned away from this unknown woman who was behaving toward him as if she were truly his wife. He was relieved to return to the synagogue, where he could sit among the congregation of Warsaw citizens and say his prayers quietly and think. He felt an enormous need to think about this strange similarity between Chelm and Warsaw.

But he was not to have the peace he needed, not even in the house of prayer. As he entered, the men stopped praying and crowded around him, all talking at once. "How could you walk to Warsaw and back to Chelm in such a short time?" was the question he heard most clearly.

By now, Getzel was really annoyed. "Stop being rude and asking silly questions!" he rebuked them. "You know you are the Jews of Warsaw and I am in Warsaw, since I walked all the way here today. I can prove that we are all in the capital city without a question or a doubt!"

"Well, prove it then!" cried the group surrounding him.

Getzel told them the whole story, how he stopped on his way to take a nap and how he made sure that his shoes would be pointing in the right direction when he awoke. Of course, he was in Warsaw and they were citizens of Warsaw.

It was hard to convince them, but the testimony of the shoes was not to be disputed. What a situation! They had lived in Chelm all their lives, and now they were no longer Chelmites, no longer who they thought they were. Could this really have happened to them?

They sat in the synagogue and talked about this dilemma for many hours. They huddled together and stroked their beards, their foreheads furrowed and their bodies swaying. Finally, they concluded that Getzel must be right, that they must all be in Warsaw, because their philosopher had walked there and had arrived at nightfall. The shoes pointing in their direction had to be foolproof evidence.

# Ethiopia

# 22

# ANIMAL TALES
# OF THE FALASHIM

Four of us are prepared to tell short Falasha stories that we wrote for our Hebrew class at the reception center. If you will forgive their primitive Hebrew, each of the four will narrate a very short tale.

All of the four fables are about animals. Many of our Falasha stories use animals to tell how we felt living in a strange land among strangers who were stronger than we were and who ruled over us despotically. It was safer to hide the true meaning of the tales by using the plight of animals as symbolic of our own condition.

Since we could not express our feelings openly, we found relief from our suffering in telling these fables. In almost every one, a small, weak animal frustrates the evil intention of a stronger, bigger animal. By outwitting him, the little fellow saves his own life and shares his triumph with his friends.

## THE CALF AND THE HEN

A calf, which was tied by rope to a hook in the barn, managed to free itself and stole outside to join its mother and feed at her teats.

A hen saw this happen and told the master of the house about the escape.

The calf remonstrated with her, saying, "Was it your business that I broke my tether and went out to nurse at my mother's teats? It must have been jealousy that made you tell the master."

The hen responded to the calf, "It was not out of jealousy that I did it, my dear. On the contrary, it was because I knew that if the master were to find his calf missing from the barn, he would give orders to slaughter the hen in its place."

## THE TIGER AND THE GAZELLE

Once upon a time, a tiger and a gazelle romped together as children and remained good friends after they grew up. They often went to the stream side by side to refresh themselves with the cool running water.

The tiger said to the gazelle, "Let's always be friends. Let's make an agreement that we'll be pals forever and that we'll never hurt each other!"

The gazelle looked up at him with her soft eyes and said, "Yes, I would like that very much."

Then the tiger asked, "What will the punishment be if one of us should break the agreement?"

The gazelle answered, "Well, whatever the punishment, it will pass to our children and it won't be inflicted upon us."

The tiger was pleased with the gazelle's response. The two friends nuzzled noses to seal the agreement.

A year passed. One day they were drinking water together, standing side by side in the stream. The tiger felt hungry.

He looked at the gazelle and thought, "I am going to eat her. After all, the punishment will pass to my children and won't be inflicted on me!"

So he picked a fight with the gazelle. He grumbled, "You are dirtying my water!"

The gazelle trembled, because she suspected that he had decided to eat her. "How can I dirty the water you are drinking," she asked, "when I am standing downstream from you? Don't make excuses. You know you are planning to eat me, no matter what!"

The tiger leaped at her. But there was a tree growing in the middle of the stream. He fell on the tree and hung there, caught in the branches. He struggled and struggled, but he couldn't get loose. And soon he knew that he would never get loose.

He called out to the world, "Why?! Why is this happening to me? The punishment was supposed to be on my children!"

The gazelle turned to him and smiled as she said, "Ah, but perhaps your father was bad before you, and you followed in his footsteps!"

## THE CATS AND THE MICE

A cat fell in love with a mouse and asked for her hand in marriage. The families agreed to the terms of the engagement and set a date for the wedding.

But before the nuptials, some of the cats, members of the bridegroom's family, put their heads together and agreed to destroy the mice, members of the bride's family. While accompanying the groom to the wedding, his family would suddenly, without warning, leap upon the mice waiting at the edge of the field. The bride and all her family would be devoured.

But the mice were much too clever to be caught in that trap. They also put their heads together before the wedding, and one of them said, "Who knows whether or not our prospective in-laws, the cats, are planning a sudden attack on us? We must be wise and anticipate such a catastrophe. Let us therefore dig holes that we can use as shelters in the event of such a disaster."

The mice followed this advice. In the weeks that followed, they dug many deep holes all over their field.

When the wedding day dawned, the cats set out to accompany the bridegroom to his nuptial feast, playing festive songs on their muscial instruments. On the field, the mice welcomed them, dancing to the beat of their own band. But every mouse was careful to dance near the entrance to a hole. Whenever a cat approached a mouse, it would leap gracefully to the nearest hole and escape by pirouetting into it.

As you can imagine, the wedding was a disaster. The marriage was canceled. The cats, who had failed to catch even one mouse, returned in the direction from which they had come.

From that time on cats have hated mice intensely, and mice have been profoundly wary of cats.

## THE MACAQUE, THE LION, AND THE BABOON

A macaque approached a lion and asked, "Why does a handsome, courageous lion like you walk around without shoes?"

The lion replied, "Indeed, I do long for shoes, but I have never found a pair that fits."

The macaque offered, "The baboon knows how to make magnificent shoes. I suggest that you order a pair from him."

The macague said this because he hated the baboon intensely, and hoped that the lion would devour him.

Upon the advice of the macaque, the lion went to the baboon and said to him, "I have heard said of you that you make extraordinary shoes. I want you to sew a decorative pair for me, one that will enhance my beauty and grace."

The baboon responded, "It is true that I know how to make shoes, but superb shoes such as you are requesting are made from the skin of the macaque and are sewn with his sinews."

The lion summoned the macaque and flayed off his skin. The macaque screamed in great pain. The baboon said to him, "You plotted to destroy me, but instead the evil you planned for me is visited upon you."

The lion gave the baboon the skin and the sinews he had taken from the macaque. The baboon dragged the skin to the nearby river and left it soaking in the water to soften it.

After a while the lion said, "I think it is time to remove the skin from the water. I'm sure it is soft enough for you to be able to sew a magnificent pair of shoes for me."

The baboon went back to the river and returned empty-handed. Trembling, he said, "Master lion, when I came to take the skin out of the water, I saw in the river a lion big and strong just like you. I was afraid of him and ran away."

The lion responded, "Show me the spot and I will attend to that other lion so that you will be able to take the macaque's skin out of the river."

The lion and the baboon walked together. When they were at the river's edge, the baboon showed the lion his reflection in the water. The lion jumped into the water to grab the lion he saw there, but came up with only a handful of clay. In a rage, he ran back to the baboon.

When the baboon realized that the lion had not drowned as anticipated, he said, "Accept my advice, dear sir. Only if you tie a large rock to your body will you be able to sink deep enough to grab the lion in the river."

The lion did not grasp the intention of the baboon, and said to him, "Your advice is good."

He tied a large rock to his body and again jumped into the river. This time he sank down and did not come up again.

And that is how the little baboon bested the big strong lion.

# II

# ARAB TALES

# Folktales Told
# throughout the
# Arab World

# FOREWORD

## ON THE FAIRY TALE

Almost every one of us is able to remember favorite folk-tales from our childhood. We can also still visualize the friendly face and familiar voice of the narrator who told the tale or the reader to whom we listened. When we think of the tales, we will usually remember that person; and when we think of the person, we will often remember the stories. The narrator is often a person close to us, a relative or a friend.

One of the typical images that comes to mind may be as follows: The mother, grandmother, or aunt, is seated comfortably next to the bed with a smile on her face and peace in her heart. She reaches to the blanket, making sure the child is comfortable and secure, and begins: "Once upon a time there was . . ."

The words of the tale would then come to us accompanied by only a few hints about the details. Our imagination would provide life to the words: the beauty of a princess, the ugliness of a demon, the goodness of the hero, the badness of the villain, and so on. With these custom-made characters, acts, images, and scenes, the tale is always in agreement with the way we think things ought to be. It is this atmosphere of security, contentment, and agreeableness that gives our childhood tales a lasting effect on our minds and feelings. When we grow up, these childhood tales

are typically dismissed as "kid stuff," but their impact on
us will have been accomplished.

## ON THE PRESENT WORK

In this segment of the anthology of retold folktales, Dr.
Blanche L. Serwer-Bernstein presents a sample of the traditional verbal art of the Arabic-speaking communities in
the Middle East. As indicated by some texts in this work,
in particular, "Djuha Borrows a Pot" and "A Contest in Sign
Language," the original folk narrators of the tales on which
the author's renditions are based may have been of the Moslem, Christian, or Jewish faiths. Shared traditions among
members of these religious denominations cover all walks
of life and exceed, at least in volume, areas over which differences exist.

The author groups her re-created tales in three broad
categories, based on the major theme that a tale seems to
express. Whatever the criterion for placing one text in one
category or another may be, we will always find the narrative portraying certain human values and concerns that cut
across national, religious, and language barriers.

In the first group, "Tales about Changes in Men," the
ideal that true love is not to be purchased with material
things is expressed; it is also the focus of the tale "Love in
a Garden." The importance of friendship and of trust among
friends provides the foundation for "The Folly of Jealousy."
This tale also draws attention to the fragility of many social
relations and points out that enduring friendship requires
understanding, equality, and sacrifice. In folk communities this tale, typically, tells of a female cousin who helps
her father's brother's son to decipher the enigmatic sign
language of a princess and to marry the girl, whom he really
loves.

The opinion that one should carefully examine a religious belief when that belief is being promoted by a person
with self-serving objectives is depicted in the tale "The

Prophet Who Was Not There." Other valued aspects of social life, such as hospitality and self-abnegation, are given in "Boastfulness versus True Generosity" and "Miserliness Cured."

The second and third groups, titled "Tales of Humor and Entertainment" and "A Kaleidoscope of Human Characteristics," respectively, offer a variety of topics and matters of human interest. One of these is humor. When told in oral tradition, the intent of the narrator of a humorous story is to get the listener (or the reader, in the present work) to smile or chuckle. Although each tale contains numerous other themes, eliciting laughter is the main consideration for telling it.

A genre of folktales dealing with humor is the trickster tale. As a traditional character, the trickster may be an insect (e.g., Ananse the Spider in West Africa), an animal (e.g., Bugs Bunny in American popular culture), or a human (e.g., Goha in Arab and other Middle Eastern communities). In each of these cases, the trickster is an amalgamation of contradictions: shrewdness and naivete, intelligence and stupidity, kindness and cruelty, morality and immorality, sincerity and deception, wisdom and foolishness. Despite the fact that we are raised to disdain trickery, trickster tales have considerable appeal. This is, perhaps, due to the fact that real life is a mixture of all the contradictions found in trickster tales, and although the temptation of the tricky option is always there, we are taught to choose not to take it. We may unconsciously hold a begrudging admiration and a resentment of the trickster, who always gets away with things that tempt us, but we cannot do.

Goha is a folk character recurrent in Arabic folklore who seems to have gained international fame as a trickster. Like all folktales circulating by word of mouth, the pronunciation of Goha's name and the descriptions of his sayings and actions are as varied as the languages and customs of the peoples who tell about them in the form of humorous anecdotes—for example, Djuha, Jiha, and Ch'ha. (One published collection of Ch'ha anecdotes was derived from North African Jewish-Arab sources by André Nahum, and titled *Les contes de Ch'ha*, Paris, 1977).

Some of the Goha anecdotes given in the present anthology are "Djuha and His Donkey: A Medley of Tales," which links a number of independent units dealing with Goha's bag of stinging verbal retorts and outrageous practical tricks, and "Djuha Borrows a Pot," which imparts indirectly the same moral expressed in an Egyptian folk truism that states: "As long as the greedy exists, the impostor will make a living" or in the American popular saying that warns: "If it is too good to be true, it probably is." So, in spite of their outrageous nature, trickster tales have a moral lesson to teach.

Another component of these two chapters is the formula tale, a genre that emphasizes the way a tale is constructed. Because such tales are not easy to tell and require considerable skill to perform, many folk narrators refer to them as puzzles.

Two of the puzzles included in this work have a pronounced humorous nature; these are "The Beetle Who Wished to Get Married" and "Friendship: Loyalty Transcends Death." Both tales personify nonhuman elements of the social and physical worlds in which we live. The latter is known in folk communities as "The Virgin's Louse," or "The Louse and Her Husband, the Flea (Pilgrim Abu-Ammar)." It illustrates the feeling of empathy that we may observe among the various elements of the environment: insects, plants, animals, wells, hills, and people. The tale also indirectly expresses the viewpoint that such sentiments, though admirable, should not be carried to an extreme.

A third theme addressed in these two chapters is the importance of communication among individuals and groups. Such a process is typically referred to in folk traditions as give-and-take, or simply, "To say, and to listen." Modern life has made this art—conversing for the sake of being with someone for whom we care—a rare thing. Two stories, placed in separate categories, illustrate how lack of communication, or miscommunication, produces unexpected and undesirable results. These are "A Contest in Sign Language" and "Total Confusion: Why Learn to Speak?" Fortunately, in both humorous narratives the results of the failure were benign.

## ON THE TALES AND LITERARY TRADITIONS

Readers, particularly those who have read the fairy tales attributed to the Brothers Grimm and to Hans Christian Andersen, may recognize some of the stories in the present work. For example, "The Prophet Who Was Not There" may remind readers of "The Emperor's New Clothes." The narrative "A Fairy Tale: Three Sisters, a Prince, and a Magic Pot" may sound very much like "Aladdin and His Magic Lamp" and "Cinderella." The reason for the similarities is that the tales we identify with the Grimms and with Andersen (or with Walt Disney movies) are, like the present ones, represented folktales. Oral traditions have always served as the great source from which creative novelists and poets have derived their materials.

## THE TELLER AND THE TALES

Although a tale may be told by any person, women are the main narrators of the fairy tale, especially the ones that are rich in fantasy and imagination, and those revolving around the supernatural (students of folklore label such narratives magic tales). Moreover, certain fantasy tales seem to be narrated almost exclusively by women, regardless of the narrator's social rank, religious affiliation, or level of education. Examples of such female-bound stories in the present anthology are "The Folly of Jealousy," "Friendship: Loyalty Transcends Death," and "The Beetle Who Wished to Get Married." Current research shows that these delicately textured accounts are narrated almost exclusively by females. Thus, it is not surprising that our present tale-teller, Dr. Serwer-Bernstein, found them appealing and worthy of her creative attention.

## CONCLUSION

Most folktales are hundreds, even thousands, of years old. They embody the diverse experiences of a people throughout the ages. Like life itself, they contain the ingenious as well as the stupid, the peaceful as well as the warlike, the humorous as well as the tragic, the admirable as well as the despicable. Folk narrators recognize this fact and select what they tell in light of the composition of their audience. One raconteur refused to tell a fairy tale to an outsider (the present writer) because she viewed it as "defamatory and disruptive to good relations." Thus, the importance of tales lies in considering them in their totality and with reference to how they are used.

Likewise, judging relationships among peoples and nations only in terms of the events of a short period often leads to inaccurate conclusions, particularly when these relations reach back in time for thousands of years. Tobie Nathan concludes the preface to André Nahum's book of Goha tales by stating: "By recalling the folklore shared by Jews and Arabs, perhaps we would be recalling as well, that these two peoples have known how to cry and smile together, during the course of the long centuries of their coexistence."

Innumerable cases expressing the same attitude of "normal" coexistence can be cited from all walks of life on both sides. Perhaps the words with which street performers in Egypt (who tell stories of a different sort) open their acts indicate the general feeling of a member of one group toward members of the "other." Before beginning a show, the performer addresses the spectators, who form a circle around him (or her): "Mohammed is Prophet, Jesus is Prophet, and Moses is Prophet. And every one of you who follows a prophet should bless him." Simple as it is, this practical suggestion takes into consideration the diversity of beliefs among the viewers and the importance of these beliefs. It calls for adhering to one's own faith and at the same time respecting the faiths of others.

This anthology by Dr. Serwer-Bernstein is written with considerable thought, artistry, and perceptiveness. It is entertaining and is a valuable addition to the library of literary folktales.

Hasan El-Shamy

# DEAR READERS

You wonder and even boldly ask why I have spent so many hours reading Arab folktales. A fair question. I have pondered the reason myself.

This reading adventure started many years ago, when, in my enthusiasm for fairy tales, I discovered *The Arabian Nights*. When that phase was superseded by other enthusiasms, books about horses and other animals, and then by romantic stories, I retained in my imagination all the color, the adventure, and the magic of the rides on Arabian carpets, the calling forth of genii imprisoned in bottles, and the spirits freed by rubbing magic lamps.

When I met real Arabs in Israel and heard their folktales and learned their dances, I became entranced by the warmth and color of their culture. During one of my visits in Jerusalem, I spent some time reading Arab folktales. I continued my search in the Harvard library during my years in Cambridge. But the real thrust began in the Forty-second Street branch of the New York Public Library, the most congenial and helpful place in the world, in my opinion, to read anything.

By that time, the thought had come to me that a book containing Arab and Jewish folktales would be symbolic of the coexistence of the two peoples. I began my search for stories that would be different from the Arabian Nights type of fairy tales, and would introduce the warmth and color and folksiness of the Arab culture to the American public.

I read many old folktales before selecting the eighteen that I felt I could tell in my own fashion. I hope you enjoy reading them as much as I enjoyed finding them and telling them to you through the medium of this book.

# Tales about Changes in Men

# 23

# HOW BIG IS BIG?

O nce there was a huge giant who lived in the time of
Noah. Ouj was his name, and he was the son of
Anak. (May the peace of Allah rest on Anak's soul
as the clouds rest on the summit of Mount Sunnin!)

Ouj, son of Anak, was so tall that when the flood covered the earth it reached only to his knees. He had no need
for the ark as protection against the rainwater that inun-
dated all other living beings that roamed the earth.

When hungry he would thrust his hand into the sea,
take out a fish, and bake it in the rays of the sun. When
thirsty he emptied the nearest well in one gulp.

As he walked, he stepped over tall trees as an ordinary
man would step over the grass and flowers of the fields. By
taking a few steps he could travel great distances, covering
the face of the earth in less than a day.

Lakes and rivers put no obstacles in his path. The deepest oceans did not reach his waist, and the largest lake
hardly covered his knees.

That is how tall Ouj, son of Anak, was. Three hundred
cubits to an inch was his height! And he began to think of
himself as great as he was tall.

As time passed and he met no other giant bigger and
greater than he, Ouj's pride grew until he looked up to
Heaven and haughtily addressed Almighty God, "Oh God,
is there anyone in the world bigger and greater than I?"

And God answered him saying, "Don't let pride distort your view of the world. Many of my creatures on this earth are greater than Ouj!"

The boastful giant bowed his head in disbelief and disappointment, for he had begun to think of himself as the tallest and greatest giant of all time.

Then Ouj, son of Anak, could not rest until he had met someone greater than himself. He set out and walked the length and breadth of the earth, through forest and field, over tall trees and bushes, splashing in lakes and rivers in his search for someone greater than himself.

Days and months passed. All Ouj encountered were ordinary men, who, when they spied him from a distance, fled before him, fearing that he might tread upon them and crush them.

Then one day, as the sun was sinking beyond the western horizon, Ouj came upon a queer-looking formation in the earth, a mountain in the shape of a man's foot. He was tired from the long day's journey, and he sat down in the shade of this promontory to rest. He soon fell asleep.

It was a cold night, but Ouj slept comfortably because of the heat he felt coming from the boot-shaped mountain.

In the morning, he arose and walked several miles. To his surprise, he came upon another mountain just like the one that had protected him with its shade during the heat of the day before and had warmed him at night. Two promontories unbelievably alike situated a few miles apart!

"Not a usual sight" he thought.

As he wondered about these two mountains, both shaped like a man's foot, he felt a violent tremor. An earthquake? The movement of the two high formations of earth threw him violently from one mountain to the other, although they were miles apart.

He rebounded back and forth between the two as the mountains moved closer together. Finally, it became clear that they were two enormous feet that supported a body arising above them to a height so remote that he could hardly see the end of it.

Whatever this was, it seemed to extend as high as the sky. Ouj could finally discern the head of an enormous giant on top of a huge body attached to the two foot-shaped mountains.

Ouj felt tiny, so small, indeed, that it was difficult for him to make his presence known to the gigantic creature who towered above him. He gesticulated wildly and shouted at the top of his voice. The giant was so tall he did not notice, since only a faint cry could have reached his ears at that distance.

Ouj's arms were flailing crazily about, his knees trembling with fear. At last the huge giant bent down and picked up the terrified Ouj in the palm of his hand as a man might hold a locust or a fly to examine it closely.

Realizing finally that Ouj was a creature with language like himself, the giant asked him in a booming voice what he wanted. Ouj was too frightened to respond. He remained trembling in the hand of the huge creature, wishing to run away but unable to.

Finally, Ouj plucked up enough courage to ask, "Who are you, great giant, and what has brought you to this part of the world, where I have lived since birth? I have never seen the likes of you before!"

The great giant replied, "I am a shepherd boy and I have a brother older and bigger than I. We lived with our parents, until one day we disobeyed our father, who became angry. He put each of us in his sling and swinging it around his head a few times, flung each of us in a different direction. My brother fell far to the west and I landed here in the east."

This huge giant still thought of himself as a shepherd, not as a great giant. He was just a peasant boy whose father, much larger, could fling him a long distance in a slingshot.

He would have to adjust to his life in this new location. He needed a friend, as did Ouj. The two became constant companions.

From that time to this, Ouj, son of Anak, never again boasted of his greatness. He knew deep in his heart that there would always be someone greater than he.

# 24

# LOVE IN A GARDEN

In ancient times, there was a girl named Lulua who was slim and lovely and sweet of limb, her face like a lit-up moon scented with musk, her skin soft and golden, tinged with roses. The girl Lulua sat in her garden beside the river and played music on her *rabab* and sang, and scattered crumbs to the doves.

One day it happened that a youth named Telal was out hunting with his hawk, and he directed the hawk at a dove. The dove flew off to the garden of the girl Lulua, seeking refuge in the trees. Before it could reach the protection of the leaves, the hawk swooped and the dove fell at the feet of the girl Lulua, the hawk tearing at its breast. The girl Lulua wept at the death of the dove.

The youth Telal burst into the garden pursuing the hawk, which returned to him and perched on his arm. The dove lay dead among the flowers at the girl's feet.

Then Telal saw the girl Lulua, and his heart turned to fire, for never before had he seen such beauty.

But the girl Lulua was sad and angry. She said, "Take your hawk and go, and never come back to my garden again!"

Telal fell on his knees and implored her, "Let me be your friend, let me visit with you in your garden, for being with you is more important to me than water to a man dying of thirst."

And the girl Lulua turned from him and said, "No, go and never come back!"

The youth Telal took his hawk and left the garden, but his heart was heavy and sad. He thought, "She is angry with me because my hawk slew her dove. I will bring her more doves; then she will be pleased and look kindly upon me."

The youth Telal took bird lime and nets and traps and for ten days he hunted doves. The girl Lulua sat in her garden, but no doves came to her for food, since they had all fallen into Telal's traps.

Soon the boy Telal came into the garden carrying a great cage, crowded with a hundred doves. He fell on his knees before the girl and pleaded, "Please accept these doves, and my friendship and love with them. I cannot live any longer without seeing you."

But the girl Lulua said, "No!" And she turned her face from him, for she was very angry. "These doves came to my garden freely and sat at my feet and ate my crumbs. How then can you give them to me? Release them into the air! Then take your cage and go!"

The youth Telal released the doves and departed, but his heart was sad. He could neither sleep nor eat. He stopped hawking and hunting, and sat in his house dreaming of the girl Lulua.

He thought, "Since I cannot give her doves, how else can I please her? I shall give her a golden hoopoe bird, to bring her happiness, that her heart may turn toward me."

He took his traps and lime and went into the hills, and stayed there for many months. Finally, he caught a golden hoopoe and put it into a cage.

He went to the garden and fell on his knees before the girl Lulua, and said to her, "Take this golden hoopoe and allow me to be with you and kiss your hand. I implore you."

He showed the cage to the girl, but the hoopoe was sad at being caged, and it fell down dead.

Then the girl Lulua cried, "How can you give me the

birds of the skies? Go, and stay far away from here, and let that which is free remain free!"

The youth Telal was saddened by her answer, and he took his cage and left the garden.

He went home and, in his unhappiness, thought, "Since I have no luck with birds, and since her name is Lulua, which means 'pearl,' I'll give her pearls, which I am sure will please her."

The youth Telal became a pearl diver, and he dived every day for months, until he had amassed a huge bag of pearls. He returned to Lulua's garden and, dropping on his knees before her, placed the pearls at her feet.

He pleaded with Lulua, "Please accept my gift of pearls and allow me to remain with you and walk with you in your garden."

The girl persisted in her rejection of Telal and said, "No! I want you to go away and take your pearls with you."

Telal took the bag of pearls and went slowly and sadly home. He thought in his misery, "Since I cannot succeed with doves or hoopoe birds or pearls, perhaps I should try gold."

He set sail for a distant land known for its gold, and worked there many months until he had earned enough gold to fill a large bag.

With great longing in his heart, he returned to his native land and to the garden of the girl Lulua. When he saw her, he fell on his knees and said, "Please accept this gold and let me walk with you among these beautiful trees and flowers and along this quiet river."

Again, the girl's response was, "No! Take your gold and go away."

Telal, in despair, returned to his house, wept, and thought, "Since I cannot win her with doves or hoopoes or with pearls and gold, I should try ambergris, for it is the most valuable thing in the world."

The youth Telal set sail again, this time in a whaling ship. When the crew came upon a whale and slew it, he filled a large jar with ambergris.

Again he went to the garden and stood before the girl
Lulua. He begged her, "Take this ambergris and let me sit
beside you on the bench under the tree."

But the girl answered, "No! Go away and do not return!"

Then Telal decided to ask advice from a wise old woman.
"I love the girl Lulua and cannot live without her. I have
offered her birds and pearls and gold and ambergris. There
is nothing left in the world to offer her, and still she answers 'No!' I am in despair."

The old woman laughed at his words and said, "Look
around at the beasts in the forest and in the meadow. Then
ask yourself what they do to find love."

Telal did not understand the words of the old woman.
He walked in the forest, thinking, "There is nothing for me
to do but to end my life, for life is impossible without the
girl Lulua."

Suddenly, there appeared in the thicket two graceful
gazelles walking side by side, softly brushing against each
other. They stopped from time to time to nuzzle each other
with their soft noses.

The boy Telal watched the gazelles and their love, and
thought how beautiful it was. They simply loved each other,
and there were no gifts or pleading for love.

Telal looked up to the trees and there sat two doves on
a branch. They rubbed bills and cooed gently to each other,
their bodies softly touching. The boy watched the birds and
their love, and thought how beautiful it was.

Then he remembered Lulua and her angry "No!" when
he gave her the doves and the hoopoe bird, the pearls and
the gold and the ambergris.

Telal asked himself, "Did the gazelle implore the gazelle
and give her gifts? Did the dove implore the dove and give
her gifts? Perhaps, if I want to hold the girl Lulua close to
me, I need only walk by her side and let her feel my love."

The youth Telal saddled his horse and galloped to the
garden. He stopped in front of the girl Lulua, dismounted,
and said simply, "Let us take a walk together so that we
may get to know each other."

Then Telal and Lulua walked side by side along the river, under the trees, and amidst the flowers of the girl Lulua's garden. Underneath the shimmering leaves, they talked of anything that interested them, but not at all about hunting or hawking or netting doves or hoopoes or gathering pearls or gold or killing whales for their ambergris.

When Telal said good-bye to Lulua and returned to the town, he met the old woman. She saw his happiness and said to him, "Now you know what the gazelle knows and what the dove knows."

# 25

# MISERLINESS CURED

If you repeat after me the word *Haroun-ar-Rashid*, you will be saying the ancient name of the once beautiful city of Baghdad. Many stories have been told about this glorious city, and many films have featured the adventures of its ancient princes, as well as its thieves and criminals.

The tale I'd like to relate to you now is about Abu Kasim, a very wealthy man well known in Haroun-ar-Rashid. You wlll find this hard to believe, but the well-to-do Kasim was famous not for his generosity or kindness but for his miserliness and meanness.

He was ruthless in business dealings. He never gave to the poor and showed no love for his fellowman. He was so stingy that he wore the same clothes day after day: a pair of old patched trousers, a threadbare aba, or robe, left to him by his grandfather, and a turban so faded and dirty that it was imposslble to tell its original colors.

If you looked down at his feet, you would see the most curious part of Abu Kasim's costume. His shoes, which had originally been quite unremarkable like those worn by any citizen of Haroun-ar-Rashid, were now heavy with unsightly patches. Every cobbler in the city had tried his art on these shoes. By now, with patch upon patch and sole upon sole, the shoes had trebled in weight. Soon anything that was heavy and clumsy or out of shape was said to be "like the shoes of Abu Kasim."

But that is not the end of my story, for a strange series of mishaps occurred to Abu Kasim's shoes. Then the words "like the shoes of Kasim" took on a new meaning: something unlucky!

This is the way it all happened:

One day Abu Kasim was strolling in the huge central bazaar on the street of the spice merchants, enjoying the wonderful odors and the array of multicolored bottles.

Suddenly, he was stopped by Moussa, a business acquaintance, who wished to curry Kasim's favor. With a great show of secrecy, Moussa whispered, "Would you like to make a small investment that will triple in value?"

This suggestion, as you can imagine, appealed to the miser, who expressed great interest in it.

Moussa resumed, "I have just learned that last week a glazier from Aleppo brought to Haroun-ar-Rashid a camel-load of crystal bottles of the finest quality and workmanship. He has sold all but a few dozen, and these he must sell today at a sacrifice, because sad news has reached him here that his daughter is ill at home. He has already arranged to return with the caravan that leaves for Aleppo tomorrow. Hurry to him now and you will be able to strike a good bargain."

Abu Kasim was not a man who would miss an opportunity to make a profit. He rushed to the Aleppan, bargained to the last piaster, and bought the bottles at a considerable loss to the seller.

The very next week again Abu Kasim was walking through the street of the spice merchants in the bazaar. Another acquaintance, Yusuf by name, stopped to tell him of a perfume dealer who had transported a large quantity of precious perfumes from his factory in Nisibim to Haroun-ar-Rashid. The merchant had disposed of all but a few gallons, which he would have to sell at half-price because he needed the money desperately to return to his dying father.

Abu Kasim immediately decided to take advantage of the situation. He had the beautiful crystal bottles, empty, and here was the perfume, cheap! He would fill the empty bottles with the perfume and sell them at a price that would triple the profit on both.

Again he bargained down to a price that represented a great loss to the seller. He filled his crystal bottles with the precious attar and put them back on his shelves to wait for an opportunity to demand the highest possible price. He was proud of his keen business acumen and happy in anticipation of his profits from these business deals.

How could Abu Kasim possibly foresee the bad luck fate had in store for him? His evil fortune started in a public bathhouse.

Once a year Abu Kasim indulged in the luxury of a bath. As the time for his annual bath approached, he sighed in resignation and finally entered the public bathhouse to get it over with.

While he was undressing in the outer court, he recognized an old business associate who eyed Abu Kasim's shoes with disgust and said, "It seems to me, Abu Kasim, that it is high time you bought yourself a new pair of shoes!"

Abu Kasim looked lovingly at his faithful old shoes and answered, "You may be right. Yet I feel that these shoes will last me a long while, a very long while, and will give me many more years of wear."

It was precisely at that moment that the Kadi of Haroun-ar-Rashid himself came for *his* bath. He left his elegant clothes on the bench not far from Abu Kasim's disreputable garments.

Soon a clean and refreshed Abu Kasim emerged from his bath. He looked for his old faithful shoes, but they were no longer where he had left them. In their place rested a handsome pair made of new red cordovan leather.

The old miser was happy, for it occurred to him that the man who had criticized his shoes had left him a present to prove his point. Abu Kasim pulled on the new red pair and left the bathhouse, blessing his friend for his generosity.

He had been gone only a few minutes when the Kadi, also clean and refreshed, came out of his bath to dress. He looked for his shoes, but they were nowhere to be found. Instead, tucked away in a corner behind the bench were the enormous heavily patched shoes of Abu Kasim.

Holding them up in disgust between his thumb and forefinger, the Kadi flung them away and cried angrily, "These belong to the old miser, Abu Kasim. Every dog in Haroun-ar-Rashid knows them! Did the dirty old miser dare to steal my shoes?"

Then, pulling himself to his full height in his bare feet, the indignant Kadi roared, "Go quickly and bring the miserable creature to the courthouse to appear before me. I will teach him to rob the Pillar of the Law, the Kadi himself, of a new pair of cordovan leather shoes!"

Soon Abu Kasim stood before the Kadi in court. Puzzled and embarrassed, the miser declared his innocence. "It was a mistake, Your Excellency, a mistake, I assure you."

His defense was drowned in a roar of laughter in which all the spectators joined. The idea that Abu Kasim could mistake anyone else's shoes for his own was ridiculous.

Abu Kasim was given the choice of paying a fine of five hundred dinars or of going to jail. Although it nearly broke his heart, he paid the fine, put on his unsightly shoes, and left the jeering crowd at the courthouse.

He no longer felt kindly toward his faithful old shoes. He decided to part with them forever.

The very next morning he bought a new pair of shoes. In the dark of the night, he flung his old shoes into the Tigris River, murmuring, "Good riddance!"

The next day a party of fishermen happened to lower their net at that very bend in the river. When they began to pull in the net, they found it very heavy, They exchanged happy glances; this surely must be a good catch.

"All together, heave!" they shouted, dragging the weighty net out of the water. They gathered eagerly around it, wondering how many big fish they had caught. Among the

frayed meshes of the net, they saw two ugly objects familiar to them all.

"Abu Kasim's shoes!" they all shouted with one voice,
and bitterly called down Allah's wrath on the miser.

One of them took the old shoes and flung them through
the window of Abu Kasim's house on the side near the riverbank. The shoes sailed across the room onto the shelves
where the miser had so carefully arranged his colorful crystal bottles of perfume. Down they crashed, spilling their
precious contents over the floor.

Abu Kasim rushed into the room and found the floor
covered with the sweet-smelling wreckage. Among the
shards of crystal lay his monstrous water-soaked shoes,
come home like a curse to roost.

Abu Kasim wailed and tore his hair. He lamented his
lost hope for a big profit from his purchases.

He regretted the day he had set foot in the unlucky
shoes. He called them names that cannot be repeated, and
said things to them that can be understood only in Arabic.
Not until his outburst of anger and grief had subsided did
he hit upon another idea for getting rid of the luckless shoes.

He decided to bury these hideous objects at midnight
outside the city where no one would ever find them.

In the dark that night he slithered through the deserted
streets of Haroun-ar-Rashid to a lonely spot outside the city
wall, and started to dig.

A few minutes later, the guards on their rounds spied
him. "Oho, there!" they cried, as they surrounded the unfortunate miser. "So, you're digging for treasure? We shall
see what the Kadi says!"

Now, everybody knows, and you must know, too, that
all buried treasure has always been the exclusive property
of the Caliph. Those who chance to stumble upon it must
by law bring it to the palace at once; if he keeps it, he will
die. It seemed clear that someone digging in the ground secretly in the shadow of night meant to defraud the Caliph
of his property.

So it was that Abu Kasim stood again before the Kadi of Haroun-ar-Rashid. The judge listened to the story told by the miser, that he had crept forth in the middle of the night to bury his old shoes outside the city limits.

Unconvinced, the Kadi increased the size of Abu Kasim's fine from five hundred to a thousand dinars for his impertinence in telling such an incredible tale.

Abu Kasim felt robbed of his life's blood. The wretched miser left the court, wondering how he would manage to rid himself of his accursed shoes, which were making his life miserable.

He forgot how fond he had been of them. He forgot how long and faithfully they had served him. Seeing an open manhole, he hurled the heavy shoes into the sewer with all his might, crying, "May Eblis wear you in Gehenna, where you belong!"

Abu Kasim felt exuberantly happy. Gone were the shoes that had caused all his troubles. At last he could settle down and make up for the losses they had inflicted on him.

But that is not how the story ended. Instead, his shoes went sailing down the sewer main until they came to a narrow section of pipe, where their bulkiness prevented them from getting through.

The water in the sewers of Haroun-ar-Rashid began to rise and finally poured out from all the manholes until at last all the streets, boulevards, and squares of the city were flooded with the evil-smelling liquid. The maintenance men worked night and day until they finally found the spot where the pipes were clogged. And the miscreants again were Abu Kasim's shoes!

The city was in an uproar. Everybody clamored for vengeance against the old miser who had caused so much unpleasantness to them all.

This time Abu Kasim felt the full weight of the law. The Kadi decided that the shoes were responsible for all the damage caused by the flood. The owner of the shoes was to pay a fine large enough to cover the cost of cleansing and rehabilitating the entire city.

The miser Abu Kasim was forced to dig up every bit of gold he had hidden beneath the flagstone of his courtyard. He remained without a dinar to his name.

Stunned by his impoverishment and blinded by rage and sorrow, Abu Kasim made his way home through the streets of Haroun-ar-Rashid carrying his filthy, despised footwear.

How was he to get rid of these accursed shoes? He had tried to drown them and they had risen from their watery grave. He had tried to bury them in vain. Even Haroun-ar-Rashid's slimy sewers had spewed them out in disgust.

What was left for him to do? He finally decided to try fire. He would burn them, strew their ashes, and be rid of them forever. Calling them all the horrid names in his vocabulary, he flung his shoes, still wet and slimy, on top of the flat roof of his house to dry.

But the spell of Abu Kasim's evil fate had not yet spent itself.

On the roof next door, his neighbor's little dog was playing in the sun. It saw Abu Kasim's shoes fall with a thud and, as little dogs will, delighted in this new toy. It leaped onto Abu Kasim's roof. With merry little growls and grunts it began to push and pull the old shoes. In its innocent play, the little dog dragged the shoes to the edge of the roof.

Down they catapulted! Unfortunately, they landed on a woman who happened to be walking on the street below. She was knocked unconscious and taken to the city hospital.

The angry crowd dragged Abu Kasim from his house. Once more the unfortunate man stood before the Kadi in court.

This time, to atone for what his shoes had done, all that he had left—the very house that sheltered him—was taken away from him. The poor miser had nothing but his faded aba, his dirty turban, his new shoes in which he stood, and, of course, the wretched old patched shoes that had been returned to him once more.

All his life Abu Kasim had slaved to amass great wealth. He had given nothing to the poor and needy. He had never offered a gift to a friend. He had spent nothing on himself until he could no longer avoid doing so. He had haggled and driven as sharp a bargain as he could, dropping his purchase money into the seller's hand with a sigh and a groan as each coin slipped from his fingers.

And his shoes, which symbolized his lifelong love of money, had betrayed him. He was enraged at those filthy old shoes, patched and repatched!

His voice trembled with grief and anger. "Your Honor," he said to the Kadi, "I have sinned against the Prophet's law, which tells us to be charitable and to place good deeds above gold. Now that I must begin life all over again, I shall not make the same mistake.

"I beg you to grant me the protection every good Moslem has the right to request. I have two vicious enemies in all Haroun-ar-Rashid, two enemies that have ruined me—my two accursed shoes! Allah be my witness, I dread them as I do Eblis the Accursed One. I am afraid to spend another moment in their company. I cast them off and renounce them!

"I ask only one favor of the court: that you give me a paper signed and sealed by your own hand, stating that I am no longer the owner of these shoes and am not responsible for any evil they may cause!"

Amid the laughter of the onlookers, the Kadi granted Abu Kasim's request. The cured miser walked off with his precious paper. His mind was at peace. Although he had nothing in the world, he was at long last rid of his unlucky shoes. He was a happier man than he had been in a very long time.

# 26

# BOASTFULNESS VERSUS TRUE GENEROSITY

Once there was a great and famous Caliph of Baghdad, Haroun-al-Rashid, who was well liked by his people, but he had one great fault known to all: he boasted that no man alive gave as splendid gifts as he did. His pride and arrogance came between him and his people.

This worried his chief minister, the Grand Wazir Jafar, whose loyalty to the Caliph provided the courage to broach the subject with the ruler.

After kissing the ground three times at the Caliph's feet, Jafar said, "O Commander of the Faithful, forgive your humble servant Jafar for daring to remind you that a true believer is always humble before Allah. He never boasts of his riches or his generosity. It would be nobler of you, O Caliph, to leave it to your subjects to praise you for your generous gifts.

"Forgive me for pointing out that you are not the greatest giver. There is a young man in the city of Basra who gives more splendid gifts than the most powerful king, and he does not boast of them."

The Caliph's face became red and his eyes flashed his fury. "Miserable Wazir," he roared, "don't you know that to tell me a lie is a crime punishable by death?"

"I speak the truth," answered Jafar, prostrating himself before the Caliph. "When I was last in Basra, I was the guest of this fine young man, Abu Ahmad, and I was astonished at his generosity and his humility. He must have endless treasures of a most unusual quality, for his gifts are unique, and he gives them freely. If you do not believe me, O Caliph, send a messenger to Basra to test my words."

The Caliph was so furious that he could not speak. He signaled to his guards, who grabbed hold of Jafar and dragged him off to prison.

The Caliph stalked out of the room and went straight to the apartment of his Queen, Zobeide, where he flung himself down on a sofa without uttering a word.

The Queen was upset when she saw how angry he was, but she was too wise to ask him what was wrong. She poured him a glass of rose-scented water and murmured, "The blessing of Allah be with you. Some days are filled with gloom and some with joy. May all your days be filled with happiness, my lord."

Her sweet voice had a calming effect on him, as always. He drank the rose water slowly. In a relaxed mood, he told her all about his altercation with his Wazir.

The clever Queen understood that Jafar's life was in danger. She did not think it wise to defend him at that moment to her irate husband. She did agree, however, that a messenger to Basra might easily discover the truth about the young man's generosity.

"That is only just," admitted the Caliph, "and I do want to be fair. Jafar has always been faithful to me and loyal to our country. I will not have him hanged until I am certain about the truthfulness of his report. But since there is no one else I can trust, I will dress in disguise and go to Basra myself."

That very day, the Caliph set out alone by camel from Baghdad to Basra, dressed as a traveling merchant. Allah took him safely to Basra, where he went directly to the best khan in the city.

The Caliph immediately inquired of the innkeeper, "Is it true that there is in Basra a young man named Abu Ahmad known for his wealth and his generosity, who gives more splendid gifts than any king?"

"Indeed there is," replied the innkeeper. "The blessings of Allah be on him! If I had a hundred mouths and the same number of tongues in each mouth, I would not be able to give his generosity the full praise it deserves."

The Caliph was still incredulous. After seeing to the care of his camel, he had his supper and retired for the night.

After breakfast the next morning he set out on foot. On the way he stopped off to ask a shopkeeper in the bazaar the way to Abu Ahmad's house.

"If you do not know that," smiled the shopkeeper, "you must have come from far away. Abu Ahmad is better known in Basra than any king in his capital city. I will send my son to guide you."

When the Caliph reached Abu Ahmad's home, he saw a splendid palace, built of light pink marble with great doors of green jade. He said to the doorkeeper, "Go tell your master that a stranger has come from Baghdad especially to visit him."

Abu Ahmad immediately descended to the courtyard to welcome his unexpected visitor. After they had greeted each other in the name of Allah, Abu Ahmad led his guest into a hall of remarkable beauty. They seated themselves on a soft couch of green silk embroidered with gold, which extended around the four sides of the hall.

Abu Ahmad clapped his hands and twelve male attendants entered, carrying cups of agate and rock crystal, set with rubies and filled with the finest red wine. They were followed by twelve female attendants, beautiful as the full moon in a cloudless sky, bearing porcelain basins of fruit and flowers and large golden goblets of sherbet covered with cream as white as snow. The Caliph had never tasted anything so delicious, although the finest food and drink in the Eastern world were brought to his palace daily.

Abu Ahmad then led him to a second hall, more splendid than the first. There delicious fish and chicken and meats were served on golden dishes.

Finally, they went into a third chamber for desserts.

Light pastries, jam, and honey were served, followed by white and red wines in golden goblets.

As they ate, sweet singers and gifted instrumentalists entertained them. The Caliph was especially moved by the tone of the lute music, and praised the sound to Abu Ahmad.

The Caliph never expected such a meal and such a concert on earth. It all seemed to be taking place in Heaven.

Abu Ahmad excused himself politely and left the hall for a moment. When he returned he was carrying an amber wand in one hand and in the other a little tree of silver adorned with leaves of emeralds and fruits of rubies.

He set the tree in front of the Caliph, who saw that there was a golden peacock of rare workmanship perched on the top of it. Abu Ahmad touched the bird with his amber wand. It immediately stretched its golden wings and spread the jeweled splendor of its tail. Then it began to rotate quickly, sending out little jets of perfume that filled the hall with a heavenly scent. No sooner had the Caliph shown an interest and settled down to watch this wonder than Abu Ahmad carried it off.

"This is strange behavior," thought the Caliph angrily, "snatching it away before I have my fill of watching the bird. It doesn't appear as if Abu Ahmad understands how to be generous!"

Abu Ahmad came back carrying a cup carved from a single giant ruby and filled with purple wine. He gave it to the Caliph, who drank all the wine, the finest he had ever tasted. To his surprise, the cup filled itself with wine at once. He emptied it again, and once more it filled itself.

He could not refrain from asking his host, "How does this miracle happen?"

"The cup was made by a wise and holy man who knew all the secrets of nature," replied Abu Ahmad, taking the cup from the Caliph and hurrying out of the hall.

"By my life," thought the Caliph, his anger increasing. "This young man has no idea of good manners. As soon as he sees I am pleased with anything, he snatches it away. When I return to Baghdad, I will teach my Wazir Jafar to be a better judge of men and to turn his tongue around his mouth before he speaks. I had better leave before I lose my temper!"

When his host returned, the Caliph arose and said, "Abu Ahmad, I am overcome by the generosity you have shown me, an unknown stranger. Allow me to leave you to your rest, for I must not trespass further on your kindness."

The young man bowed, not wishing to detain his guest beyond his desire to remain. He accompanied the Caliph to the palace gate, where he said, "I beg you to forgive me for having given you entertainment unworthy of so delightful a visitor." They bowed to each other and parted.

The Caliph walked back to the khan muttering furiously to himself, "That young fool did nothing but show off his riches and treasures to me. Generous, indeed! I'll teach Jafar what happens to anyone who lies to me!"

He was still fuming when he reached the inn. At the gate he found a line of Abu Ahmad's attendants, each carrying on a brocaded cushion one of the desirable objects that had been displayed in the palace.

A young attendant handed the Caliph a scroll of silk paper. He unrolled it and read these words: "The peace of Allah be upon a charming guest, whose coming brought happiness! It seemed to me that you were not displeased by these objects, which I now put before you, the lute whose music you seemed to enjoy, the wine cup, and the tree. I hope you will accept them from one whose house you have honored. Abu Ahmad."

"By the honor of my ancestors!" cried the Caliph. "How I have misunderstood this young man! Where is my generosity now? It is nothing compared to his! O faithful Jafar, how right you were to rebuke me for my pride and boasting!"

He called for pen and ink and fine silk paper and wrote a note in which he described his gratitude to Abu Ahmad.

He gave it to the smallest of the attendants to deliver to his master. Then he returned with Abu Ahmad's gifts to the palace in Baghdad.

His first official act was to release Jafar from his dungeon and to give him a robe of honor to show the whole court that he was reinstated as the Grand Wazir. Then he told Jafar the story of his adventures and asked, "What can I do to reward this generous young man?"

"O Commander of the Faithful," answered Jafar, "you have confirmed that Abu Ahmad lives and behaves like a king, and is much beloved in his city. May I suggest that you make him King of Basra?"

"You are wise, Jafar," responded the Caliph. "Let the patent of royalty be drawn up for me to sign. Then, Wazir, you yourself will travel to Basra and bring Abu Ahmad here. He will be crowned in my presence so that we may rejoice together."

All this was done.

The great Caliph no longer boasted about the splendor of his gifts to others. Moreover, he spread throughout the caliphate the tale of Abu Ahmad's generosity.

# 27

# THE FOLLY
# OF JEALOUSY

Once in Iraq there were two small boys. One was the son of the Sultan, and he was called the Amir Abdulla; the other was the son of the Wazir, and his name was Mohammed. These boys were as close friends as David and Jonathan. In play and in mischief they were always together; they shared in the fun and in the disappointments of childhood.

When the time came for them to be educated, their fathers agreed to send them to the same school so that their friendship might flourish. And in the ten years of their schooling, they remained together in fun, in play, and in the inevitable mischief of school years. They bullied the younger boys, they played at archery and rode their horses, they drank wine, and they wondered about the beauty hidden behind the veils of the girls and young women who passed them by.

There was one big difference between them, however. When they finished their years of schooling, Mohammed, the Wazir's son, was well educated and knew every language spoken in the world at that time, for not only was he clever, but he had applied himself industriously to his studies. Abdulla, the Sultan's son, had learned nothing, because fun and play had been his whole existence.

What were they to do when they left school? The Amir Abdulla's father was still the Sultan and Mohammed's father

the Wazir, both still active in governing Iraq. No thought
was given to employing these two young men, the future
rulers of their country. They were left to their own devices.

It became their custom to rise at dawn, to ride their
horses into the high, dry desert, and to return in the evening. For their safety, the Sultan provided an escort of six
handsome Circassian youths armed with spears and swords.

The Amir Abdulla chafed at having to spend the day with
an armed escort. As soon as they were deep into the desert
he would dismiss the Circassians, ordering them to return
before the setting of the sun to accompany him back to the
palace.

Then he and Mohammed would spend the day basking
joyously in each other's companionship. Covering their
faces with their *kaffiyehs*, they would race their horses in
the desert sand, sending clouds of dust into the air. They
would approach every passing caravan and question the
travelers about their point of departure, the number of days
they had spent in the desert, and their destination. They
would study the plants and the animals of the desert.

This was a most fruitful and happy time for them, until
something happened that changed the course of their lives.
And it all started and ended with jealousy, an evil emotion
that caused great hardship and sorrow.

The Circassian youths assigned to guard the Amir
Abdulla became jealous of his intense friendship with
Mohammed. The guards complained to their Commander,
"The Sultan's son has no use for us and dismisses us. We
have orders to leave in the morning and return in the even-
ing. We are totally neglected, for he has eyes only for the
Wazir's son, Mohammed."

Another day they approached their Commander, again
saying, "We are sick to death of this state of affairs. We are
tired of the desert every morning and every evening. The
only solution to this attachment of the Amir Abdulla to the
Wazir's son is to kill Mohammed, and we shall do that!"

The Circassian Commander countered, "That would be

a foolish thing to do. We can get rid of him without placing ourselves at odds with the Sultan and the Wazir. Let us consult with the town witch whose success in witchcraft is renowned throughout the land. She will use her magic to disrupt the harmony that now exists between the two boys."

When the Circassian youths had explained their situation to the witch, she responded, "I'll have no problem in creating envy and dissension between the boys. Nor is it necessary to use abstruse knowledge from forbidden books to accomplish this. All I require of each of you is one dirham.

With the six dirhams that she received from the Circassian youths, she went to the market and bought powder and paint for her face, and a youthful red dress and scarf. Upon her return home, she incanted magic words as she washed her face with curdled milk and applied kohl under her makeup. Although she was an old woman of threescore and ten, she was able to make herself look, from some paces away, like a young girl of seventeen.

When the Amir Abdulla and Mohammed arrived at their usual spot in the desert the next morning, they saw a young girl dressed in an attractive red dress sitting on a mound about a hundred paces from the road. Both of them spurred their horses and raced toward her.

Mohammed reached the mound first and dismounted gracefully. He climbed by leaps and bounds up the rocky hill to its summit. To his amazement, no one was in sight on either side of the hill but a dirty old witch with toothless gums. There was nothing else in view in that whole boundless desert, where even a flea would not be able to find a place to hide in its open vastness.

As Mohammed descended slowly to where his horse was waiting, the Amir Abdulla called out to him, "Han, Han, how did you fare? Did she let you kiss her?"

Mohammed responded, "There was no girl on the mound, only an ugly old witch; it must have been a mirage that deceived us."

The Amir Abdulla was enraged because he did not believe Mohammed's story. He lost trust in his friend, as the witch had anticipated. She had sown the seeds of jealousy, distrust, and hatred.

The son of the Sultan turned toward the son of the Wazir and murmured, "Do you think I am fool enough to believe you? You did see her, and you must have taken her in your arms. Are you my friend if you lie to me? Your lie will not benefit you, for I no longer consider you my friend."

Abruptly, the Amir Abdulla turned his horse around, and, leaving Mohammed thunderstruck and devastated in the hot desert, galloped home at full speed. As soon as he arrived in his own quarters, the Sultan's son summoned the Commander of the Circassian guards. He issued harsh orders in his most authoritative voice: "Go immediately to Mohammed's room and kill him."

Although he had expected a strong reaction to the jealousy aroused by the witch, the Circassian Commander was flabbergasted at the severity of the punishment the young prince was meting out. Terrified by the success of his own plan, he bowed before the youthful Amir and dared to protest, "Mighty Amir, your wish is my command, and I do not hesitate to carry out your orders. But allow me to point out in Allah's name, that until now Mohammed has been your best friend from childhood on. Why not imprison him and wait until your anger cools down? I fear you will be saddened by the finality of his death. Give yourself the opportunity to change your mind."

Enraged, the young Amir clung adamantly to his decision and shouted, "Do as I have commanded, or you will be slain together with him!"

The Circassian Commander could not bear to kill a fine boy he had known all his life; he also feared the reaction of the Wazir at the loss of an only son. However, unwilling to go to his own death with Mohammed, the Circassian found a sick dog and mercifully put it out of its misery by stabbing it. With his sword dipped in the animal's blood, he returned to the young Amir and explained, "This is the blood of your friend, Mohammed, for I have executed your orders faithfully."

The young prince paled at the sight of his friend's blood, proof of his death.

The Circassian Commander hid Mohammed in a remote cave. He selected his most trusted attendant and assigned him the task of bringing food, water, clothes, and other necessities to the unfortunate young man.

That is not the end of this sad story.

For the Amir Abdulla was saddened by the loss of his friend Mohammed's companionship, and spent many dreary hours longing for the intimacy and playfulness of their relationship. One lonely day, he rode with his attendants into the countryside in the direction of the Persian Gulf.

He stood on a mound overlooking the vast body of water, wishing Mohammed were there to share the beautiful sight with him. As he watched the many different kinds of ships and small craft in the sunlight, he was attracted by the sight of a beautiful schooner with her sails fully unfurled, traveling as fast as an Arabian horse, faster than the wind itself.

As it flew past him, Abdulla saw standing in its bow, with hair flying, the most beautiful girl he had ever imagined, even in a dream. Her face was like the flowers of Mosul, and her skin was as pure white as the snow of the Kurdish mountains. She stood in the wind, her dress clinging to her supple body and beautiful breasts. Abdulla looked at her as she passed and felt love welling up in him.

And the girl saw Amir, a young man beautiful as the moon itself, standing on a hill overlooking the waters of the Persian Gulf. She was passing him with the speed of a bullet, but she felt the strong attraction between them and she quickly signaled to him in sign language. She placed her index finger on her eye, then on her teeth, on her navel, and finally on her head. The boat disappeared beyond the horizon.

The Amir Abdulla remembered her signals, but could

not make head or tail of them. What could they mean? And how could they lead him to her? He was certain that in doing what she did, she was informing him somehow of who she was and where she lived. Nor was the Commander of the Circassians able to provide a clue as to her meaning.

The Amir Abdulla cried out in anguish, "I must have Mohammed, son of the Wazir, for only he understands every language in the world, including all codes and sign languages!"

The Commander bowed low before the Sultan's son and murmured, "Contain your sorrow, Amir Abdulla, for you and I both know that Mohammed is irretrievable, as he is with his forefathers."

Overcome with grief, the Amir sobbed for the first time over the death of his friend, saying, "What have I done? I have lost my friend by my own decree, and now Allah punishes me, for I am losing the only woman I have ever wanted as my bride."

Now the Circassian Commander had an attendant, as you already know, who was privy to the whereabouts of Mohammed. This servant was compassionate and sympathized with both young men, the son of the Sultan immersed in tears of grief and the son of the Wazir hidden from all companionship and friendship.

The next day as usual, the servant brought food to the Wazir's son. This time, he told Mohammed of the Amir's grief and of his aching need to have his friend back. Courageously, Mohammed escaped from the cave and without permission entered the presence of his friend, the Amir Abdulla.

What a reunion ensued! The two friends embraced affectionately. And the Amir rewarded the Commander of the Circassians with a thousand dirhams for having saved Mohammed's life despite the threat of losing his own.

Now Mohammed, the son of the Wazir, easily interpreted for the son of the Sultan the message the lovely young woman had sent. The first gesture gave her name, Ayin, which means eye. Then she told who her father was, a king, for teeth are symbols of power. Third, the name of his kingdom was Surri, meaning navel. And over his palace was a pomegranate tree.

The Amir Abdulla lost no time in requesting an audience with his father, to whom he described his encounter with Ayin, the Princess of Surri. Delighted that his son had fallen in love, for he was of an age to marry, the Sultan granted him ships, sailors, and a large treasure for the journey.

Accompanied by Mohammed, the young Amir sailed for the home of the beautiful Ayin. When he arrived there, he explained his mission to the King of Surri who, impressed by Abdulla's beauty and wealth, gave his consent to the marriage.

Soon the young couple and their friend were once more on the sea bound for his home, where he continued to love her with abounding love for the rest of their lives. Allah blessed them with many sons, beautiful as moons, strong as lions, firm as spears, and brave as are Arabs all over the world.

The friendship of the Amir and the Wazir's son continued until they both matured and took over the leadership of their country as Sultan and Wazir. And they both prospered greatly.

This is a popular tale told to travelers in the desert when they stop at an oasis for tea. In the barren aridity and harshness of that terrain, the folly of jealousy becomes apparent. Since travelers are overwhelmingly men, it is often added that jealousy and envy are attributes of women, despite the fact that in this tale they are the attributes of men, both Arabic and Circassian, royal and common.

# 28

# THE PROPHET WHO
# WAS NOT THERE

Have you ever felt hunger that comes from not having a job, so that you are unable to buy food for yourself or your family? If you haven't, it will be hard for you to understand how poverty and hunger drove Badr, the Ayar, to dishonest deeds that I am about to relate to you. This tale, part of the local folklore, has come down through the generations and most people think it really happened. I myself am not sure it is grounded in fact, but after so many years, does it really matter?

The difficulty was that Badr, the Ayar, did not want an ordinary construction worker's job, for which he was well qualified and which would have solved his financial problems. He wanted a windfall bestowing riches upon him all at once, in dramatic contrast to the poverty he had suffered. He thought and thought, and finally he hit upon a way to instant prosperity.

He acted upon his idea immediately. Perhaps if he had thought a little longer he would not have done what he did. In any case, what he did was to go to a lonely, rocky field in a far-off place where nobody lived, and there he started to build a house with his own hands, using the stones he had gathered in that very field.

Several Bedouins passed by and stared at him as he worked. They asked, "Why do you build in such a remote place where the terrain is hard rock and planting is impossible?"

His response always was, "No one may know my purpose. Allah has commanded and I simply obey."

Many people became curious and whispered about him. "Is he mad?" they wondered.

He continued to build silently and told no one what his purpose was. After two months of labor, the remote stone house in the rocky field was finished. It had a front door and a rear door. Otherwise, it was quite simple, consisting of only one large room.

Now, there lived in the city a rug merchant by the name of Jafr, a very talkative man, of whom it was said that the words ran from his tongue as water runs from a cracked pot. After Badr had completed the stone house, he meandered aimlessly to Jafr's shop in the bazaar and browsed among the many-colored rugs.

It happened that the merchant Jafr, besides being a gossip, was also a very curious man, who wanted nothing more than to break the Ayar's silence about the stone house. So Jafr the carpet dealer offered Badr the Ayar a cup of coffee. When the Ayar was seated comfortably and the young messenger boy had arrived with his copper tray on which there were two small cups of Turkish coffee, Jafr offered one to his guest, also placing before him a narghile to puff at.

It didn't take long for the merchant to get the Ayar to talk about the house. "Jafr, you are the most discreet and wisest man in this city. I will confide in you, but first you must assure me that you will not disclose to anybody one word of what I tell you."

Delighted, the rug merchant Jafr gave the Ayar Badr his word.

Badr drew nearer to the merchant and whispered in his ear, "Listen, my friend, to a strange thing that happened to me. The Prophet Mohammed, on him be peace, came to me in a dream and said, 'I am coming to earth for one day, and have chosen your village to visit. I want to sit for a single day in a lonely place, and I want you to build me a stone house with two doors, back and front. In that house, I shall meet those who are noble and honorable. To the worthless sinners, I shall remain invisible. And the day is the first day of *Shaban*.'"

The merchant Jafr paled, and his eyes opened wide with amazement.

Badr the Ayar continued: "I have built the house of stone in a barren field outside the city, and it is ready for the Prophet Mohammed, on whom be peace. But it is not proper that the great prophet should have to walk on a cold stone floor. All I ask of you is the loan for a day of a handsome carpet fit for Allah's prophet to tread on."

Badr received the promise of a carpet, and in a mood of great jubilation, thanked Jafr and left the shop. No sooner was he gone than Jafr closed for the day and ran to the coffeehouse. In less than an hour everyone in town had heard the story of Badr's dream and his plans for the first day of *Shaban*. The king and the learned *sayyids* and wise men of the city were astonished. Soon they would meet the Prophet Mohammed!

On the first day of *Shaban*, the Ayar Badr received the carpet from the merchant Jafr and with his eyes turned upward toward Heaven, said, "I thank you and the Prophet Mohammed, on whom be peace, thanks you. But I beg you again to be silent about the visit of the holy Prophet Mohammed, for those who are noble and without sin will see him and those who are sinful will see nobody in the stone house."

Badr spread the beautiful carpet on the floor of the house that he had built with the stones of the isolated field.

A crowd gathered outside the house, *sayyids* or learned men, and ordinary people who were curious about who would prove to be sinful and who noble. Some stood by hoping to catch a glimpse of the Prophet Mohammed as he arrived or as he departed.

Suddenly, from inside the house there came a booming voice that announced: "Let the noble and the honorable enter one by one!"

A deep silence fell on the crowd. Then they heard the

recognizable voice of Badr, quivering with excitement in response: "We have been awaiting your arrival, O Holy One, and now we know your command. You request all who are without sin to enter, O Prophet of God, and so it shall be!"

Then Badr the Ayar emerged from the house and gazing at the huge crowd, called out, "There is nothing here for those who cannot see. Stand back, and let those who are certain of their sinlessness come forward."

Quietly, one of the wisest and most pious *sayyids* of the city stepped up, and said modestly, "I wish to enter, and I shall see what I shall see."

And Badr replied, "Go in if you wish, for I force none to enter, nor do I invite any man to enter or not to enter. You may see something remarkable or you may see nothing at all. This whole affair is not of my making, nor do I understand it. I know nothing of what is in your heart and in your past of nobility or of sinfulness."

Quietly, with head bowed in humility, the *sayyid* entered.

Once inside the large stone room, he saw two objects. On the floor was spread a beautifully woven dark red and blue carpet, in the center of which was a very large cushion, depressed in the middle as if someone were seated on it. That is all.

The *sayyid* wondered, "Can this be a trick? But Badr did not say that there would be anybody here. He said only, 'Enter and see what you will see!' Had it been a trick, he would have said, 'The Prophet of God is inside and only the virtuous will see him.'"

Then the *sayyid's* past life passed before him. He remembered one sin, and then another sin, and then a third sin. True, they were insignificant transgressions, and he had never thought anything of them. But now his heart was full of fear. He thought, "If the Prophet were truly sitting on that cushion and I did not see him, then my sins will haunt me. It will be impossible for me to live in this city with everyone knowing of my sinfulness."

He walked slowly toward the back door of the stone house and out into the sunshine, where people ran up to him and asked, "What did you see? Whose voice did we hear commanding us?"

And the *sayyid* said, "I saw the Prophet of God, on whom be peace. He talked to me and gave me wise counsel." Slowly and thoughtfully, the gentle *sayyid* headed toward the central mosque to pray.

Meanwhile at the remote stone house, another virtuous man entered expecting to encounter the Prophet, and then another and another. After a few moments, each one emerged from the back door of the house and announced, "I saw the Prophet of God, on whom be peace. I talked with him and he gave me sound advice."

Soon the King of the land heard about all that had gone on in the stone house. He joined the crowd, which parted and made way for him to enter. After a few moments he, too, emerged, saying, "I saw the Prophet of God, on whom be peace."

At the end of that long day, the first day of *Shaban*, the crowd dispersed. Badr was the last to come out of the stone house. He wended his way alone toward the city, holding both his arms in front of him as if he were carrying a precious object. He never lowered his arms.

He went directly to the King's palace, where the courtiers surrounded His Majesty and listened to the tale of his encounter with the Prophet Mohammed. Badr stood by, his arms still outstretched as if holding something precious, and waited for a chance to address his monarch. Finally, there was a pause in the King's narrative, and Badr took the opportunity to speak.

He drew near, bowed before the King, and in his most impressive manner spoke out, "O King, hear me! When the Prophet Mohammed, on whom be peace, was about to leave the stone house, he gave me his own magnificently embroidered cloak and commanded me, 'Give my cloak to the noblest person in the land who is entirely without sin, and he will reward you with ten thousand dinars.'

"I have brought the holy cloak to Your Majesty, for you are surely the person that the Prophet of God, on whom be peace, intended to receive it. Please, Your Majesty, remove the cloak you are wearing so that I may drape this cloak blessed by the Prophet Mohammed about your shoulders."

Seeing nothing in Badr's hands, the King was bewildered. All his courtiers, however, without exception, exclaimed in admiration, "What a noble cloak, fit for our virtuous King! A magnificent gift direct from the Prophet Mohammed!"

The King took off his own cloak. Badr moved his hands, draping the Prophet's cloak over the King's shoulders. After adjusting the precious cloak to hang correctly, Badr removed a hair from it. Then he gazed with utter delight at the King. Everybody joined him in expressing admiration for the way the Prophet's gift looked on the King.

The King was in a dilemma. He thought, "I cannot remain seated on my throne wearing a cloak that everybody sees except me. Why, I don't even feel it. How will I remember that I have it on?"

So he rose from his throne, explaining, "I must leave you, to hang my new cloak in a safe place, for it is not for everyday use. I'll return to my court in more appropriate clothes."

As the King departed, he carefully adjusted the cloak that was not there. Then he went up to his wife's quarters and lay down on her couch, for he could always think clearly when he was in her presence.

He said to her, "Look at this wonderfully woven cloak I am wearing. Its design and colors are magnificent, don't you agree? Please have it hung in a safe place, as it was given to me by the Prophet Mohammed, on whom be peace."

The Queen, who recognized a spade when she saw one, exclaimed in amazement, "You are not wearing a cloak. It is not right for a King to walk about in public without a cloak."

The King remonstrated with her: "If you cannot see this cloak I am wearing, you must be an evil woman. The Prophet of God, on whom be peace, gave it to me and only the noble can see it. All my courtiers and I see it well."

The Queen burst into laughter. When she could control herself well enough to speak, she said, "If what you say is true, then surely you would not see the cloak, for I know you well and am aware of your faults as well as your many virtues. Nor could any of your courtiers see it, for all are sinners and liars, and have few virtues among them!"

The King listened to the words of his Queen, whom he loved and trusted. He pondered the whole situation.

Finally, he said thoughtfully,"You may be right after all. For I did not think the Minister of Finance would see the Prophet's cloak, yet he claimed to do so. And his many sins are common knowledge.

"My good and clever Queen, bring me a glass of water. We will test whether or not there is a cloak here, for even if evil people cannot see it, the water that God provides will know for sure."

The Queen brought the glass of water. The King poured it on the cloak that was not there and the water flowed directly onto the floor.

Then the King recognized that the Queen was right. He thought ruefully, "I have declared that I saw the Prophet of God, on whom be peace, and that I talked with him, though he was not there. I have worn a cloak that was not there and declared that I saw it. Now I must pay ten thousand dinars."

He pondered the whole wretched affair, and finally knew what to do. He would return to the court and to his courtiers to carry out his plan. As he walked, he held his right hand lower than his left hand, pretending to carry a heavy weight.

He reentered the palace and was immediately surrounded by his people, Badr among them, who were curious about why his shoulders and arms were uneven as if he were carrying a weight.

He sat upon his throne as he always did when he was about to make an important announcement.

Then he spoke: "My friends and advisers, I have been doubly blessed today. Mohammed the Prophet of God, on whom be peace, came down to earth for the purpose of granting me two gifts. The first you know about, the magnificently designed cloak, which you have all seen.

"He also sent an angel, who gave me this heavy bag of gold I am carrying and said, 'The Prophet Mohammed, on whom be peace, does not want you to dip into your treasury for the ten thousand dinars reward. He declares that public money must be used solely for the good of your people. He gives you this bag of gold with which to reward the virtuous Badr.'

"Come close to the throne, good Badr, and receive your reward directly from my hands."

Badr came forward and stood before the King. He watched as His Majesty moved his hands as if counting out ten thousand dinars and heard the royal pronouncement:

"Anyone who does not see this heap of gold given by the great Prophet Mohammed, on whom be peace, is therefore evil and must be punished by death!"

When the King had finished counting the dinars that were not there, Badr thanked him graciously. He scooped up all the gold pieces he could find and filled his purse with them. He bowed, thanked the King again, and left the royal presence with his shoulders uneven and one of his arms lower than the other, pretending to carry a heavy purse of gold.

You can imagine how sad our friend Badr was. He had labored for two months to build a house, and what was his reward? Ten thousand dinars that were not there. He was still hungry, and would have to look for a job providing proper wages that would be there every payday.

# Tales of Humor and Entertainment

# 29

# WOULD YOU LIKE A JINN ON YOUR BACK?

Jinns, who have magical powers, can be big or small, good or bad, grumpy or cheerful, helpful to mortals or cruel to them, generous or selfish, serious or whimsical. I'll let you decide how to describe the Jinn in this story. The only thing I'll tell you about him is that he was unhappy about his lot in life.

But then again, so was Hamid dissatisfied with his lot. He was a poor shopkeeper who started this story by walking home one dark autumn night after a bleak, rainy day during which hardly a soul entered his shop.

Discouraged, his head hung down, he dragged his feet and mumbled to himself, "Allah, great Allah, help this poor father of four children! All I could afford to buy for dinner tonight is one loaf of bread, hardly enough to feed a hungry family. No matter how hard I try at my work and no matter how diligently I pray five times a day, my luck never changes, and I remain indigent."

He was so discouraged and angry at himself for his failure to earn an adequate living that he strayed from his usual route home and found himself in an unfamiliar wooded area outside his village. He tried to retrace his steps, frantically darting first in one direction and then in the other. Afraid that he was hopelessly lost, he panicked and fell into a gaping hole in the soggy ground.

He attempted to grasp the scrubby growth of weeds and grasses outside the hole, hoping to pull himself up. The dampness on the ground and the wet leaves in the hole made it impossible for him to prop himself up with his hands or to gain a foothold.

Realizing that he would not be able to climb out by himself, frightened and upset, he shouted in as loud a voice as he could muster, "Help! Help me out of this hole! Help me!" There was no response.

More and more frightened, he called out again and again. Finally, a raucous voice ordered, "Grab hold of my hands and I'll lift you out!"

Frantically flailing his arms around in wide circles, Hamid soon felt a pair of strong hands grasping his. The same unpleasant voice called out, "Hold on tight!" Within seconds, he was lifted up and placed on the ground outside the hole.

It was too dark for him to see who his rescuer was. He shouted, "May Allah save you when trouble befalls you! Who are you, and how can I repay you for your kindness in pulling me out of this treacherous hole?"

"I am a Jinn, a very small Jinn, even though my arms and hands are quite strong. I don't want repayment for an insignificant kindness. But I have short, weak legs and get tired when I walk. I would appreciate your holding my arm and assisting me to a place not too far away, where I'll give you a generous gift for your trouble."

Hamid was very happy to be out of the hole and on his way home. What would his wife and children do if he did not bring them at least the loaf of bread? What would they have done if he had died in that hole and never come home again? The more he thought of how important he was to the survival of his family, the more he felt he should do a good turn for the Jinn who had helped him and seemed harmless enough.

"Where shall I accompany you?" he asked.

"A mere stone's throw away, where you'll see the ruins of a house. When we get there I'll explain everything to you."

The strange pair trudged along in the damp woods, drizzle wetting them to the skin. Soon they reached a broken-down house that obviously had not been occupied in years.

"Here is where you can really help me," offered the Jinn pleasantly, "and you won't regret it. Here in this decaying wall, a great treasure lies hidden.

"Hundreds of years ago, I was sleeping on the highest branch of that tree growing out of the wall, when I was wakened by the sound of digging. I watched while a man on the ground below opened a silver casket, revealing a treasure of precious jewels and gold. He then quickly closed the casket and buried it deep in the ground.

"I realized that since a human being had hidden it, only a human could retrieve it. But most ordinary folk are fearful of Jinns and ran away as soon as I approached them. They wouldn't even listen to my story. You are the first person willing to help me dig up the the great treasure."

The shopkeeper became impatient. "How do you want me to assist you? What can I do for you?" he asked. "I'm in a hurry to get home, since my family is hungry, waiting for the loaf of bread I'm bringing them for supper."

The Jinn responded quickly, "Here is a sharp shovel. Dig in this spot until you hear metal upon metal. You will have reached a silver casket. Open it and take as much of the contents as you want. Fill your knapsack with the gold and precious stones you find here. You'll be rich and prosper for the rest of your life."

Hamid did as the Jinn had instructed, found the silver casket, and opened it. His eyes were dazzled by the gleaming jewels. At the Jinn's urging, he filled his large backpack with enough of the treasure to make him the richest trader in the *souk*.

As he was about to leave, the Jinn stopped him, saying, "There is only one more little favor I would like to ask of you. It's nothing much, just a little thing."

"What else would you like me to do? I really have to leave at once. My wife and children must be hungry and fearful for my safety by now, as it is not my custom to come home this late."

"Just a little thing," repeated the Jinn. "Since my legs are weak, I want you to carry me on your shoulders wherever you go. I won't make a fuss or even a sound. I'll just sit on your shoulders and cross my legs around your neck and hold on to your chin. I'll be no bother to you at all. And you will have plenty of treasure."

Hamid jumped up as if shot. "I can't do that for you! I would be the laughingstock of the city! Here, take your gold and jewels. I'll run home without them. I know my way from here. I don't need your help."

The Jinn retorted quickly, "Hold it! You can't do that! You're already committed to this agreement, and I won't let you get out of it. I'll imprison you together with the treasure in this hole in the old wall and you'll never be heard of again!

"You're a very foolish man. I've offered you wealth and fame for the rest of your life, and you dare to refuse me! Come, be reasonable, and I'll stick to my end of the bargain."

As he said this, the Jinn grabbed hold of Hamid, who struggled desperately to free himself. Finally, the poor shopkeeper shook his assailant off so vehemently that the Jinn fell against a large rock. Stunned, he rolled into the hole and landed on top of the silver casket.

Hamid quickly seized the rock and placed it over the hole, imprisoning the devious little fellow. After making certain that the opening was thoroughly sealed, Hamid hastily grabbed his backpack full of gold and precious stones. He ran through the woods onto the street that led to his home, where his family were waiting for him.

As you have already guessed, Hamid became a very wealthy man. He and his family prospered so well that he

became well known throughout the Arabic world as a respected and resourceful tradesman.

That sounds like the end of the story, but it's not. I wish
it were.

One of Hamid's acquaintances, Mahmoud by name, a
competitor in the *souk*, noticed this sudden rise in fortune.
Curious, he invited Hamid into his shop to enjoy a cup of
coffee and a sweet cake. As they became friendlier, Hamid's
tongue loosened and he revealed to Mahmoud the story of
the Jinn.

Hamid took special care to alert Mahmoud to the real
danger, the desire of the creature to be carried about on a
human's neck so that he would not have to walk on his
short, weak legs.

Mahmoud, already wealthy and in no need of added
riches, was nevertheless a greedy man. He begged Hamid
to tell him where the ruined old house was and how he could
find the hole under the wall. He was certain that he would
be able to control the small-sized Jinn.

One night not long after that, Mahmoud made his way
to the ruined house, where under the broken-down wall,
he found the rock Hamid had placed over the treasure and
the Jinn. Delighted, he lifted the rock and exposed the silver casket. He opened the casket and feasted his eyes on
the gold and precious jewels that sparkled in the darkness.

The Jinn was also delighted. "I've been waiting for someone to come and free me from this imprisonment. I am very
grateful to you for liberating me. You won't be sorry, because I'll make a wealthy man of you. Here, take as much
of this treasure as you wish. I see you've brought several
bags. Fill them all. And the only payment I ask is a very
small favor."

Mahmoud's eyes gleamed with avarice in the darkness.
"I'll be glad to do as you wish, O generous Jinn," said the
greedy man, as he hastily filled his bags with glistening jewels and gold. "For this gift of treasure I shall be your very
good and close friend until my dying day."

Calling out, "You're right!" the Jinn leaped on Mahmoud's shoulders and crossed his legs over the greedy man's neck, singing happily,

"Close friends we'll always be,
Your legs will always carry me;
Wherever you go I'll go too,
Whatever you do I'll also do.

You'll soon tire of our closeness
And I, too, of your moroseness;
Many quarrels may then ensue,
Your avarice you will rue.

You and I will be close forever;
No matter how hard you endeavor
To throw me off your neck and back,
The means to do that you'll always lack."

And so it was. Mahmoud paid for his greediness by becoming the laughingstock of the city and the villages for miles around. He had many years to regret his foolish decision and his unhappy fate.

# 30

# DJUHA AND
# HIS DONKEY:
# A MEDLEY OF FIVE TALES

Throughout the Arab world, stories are told about Djuha, a popular folk hero who is silly and wise, practical and philosophical, ridiculous and serious. The Djuha, or Joha, tales combine humorous simplicity with a kind of illogical logic.

Some of these tales deal with Djuha and his relationship with his donkey. I'd like to tell you a few of these Djuha-donkey stories. First I must explain the unique relationship between a *fellah*, or peasant farmer, and his donkey.

The *fellah* feels closer to his donkey than to any other coworker, yes, closer than to his dog, although both animals share his labor and both guard him against disaster, the dog by barking and the donkey by braying. His affection for his donkey is warmer than for his cat, which, although it works hard at keeping his farm free of mice, is nevertheless aloof and self-sufficient.

The *fellah* takes loving pride in his farm truck—if he is lucky enough to have one—which, like his donkey, provides transportation, recreation, and above all, a sense of power. But he loves his donkey more because beyond all this, his donkey and he are professional partners; their vocations are interdependent. And above all, his donkey has a sense of humor and fills his life with laughter and joy.

The first of the donkey anecdotes tells about the difference in the way Djuha reacted to his wife's death and to
his donkey's demise. It will illustrate the intertwining of love
and interdependence between Djuha and his donkey.

When his wife, Zahida, died, Djuha surprised his friends
by his calm demeanor. To everybody's amazement he unex-
pectedly did not weep and wail as was customary at funer-
als, although he had been happy in his marriage and had
loved Zahida very much.

Some time after that, his donkey took sick and died.
Djuha wept bitterly.

"Could he have been more affected by the death of his
donkey than of his wife?" wondered the other villagers.

One of his neighbors dared to reproach him and asked
him for an explanation of this difference in his behavior at
his two bereavements.

Djuha was quick to explain, "When my wife died, I
missed her sorely, but my friends all visited and consoled
me. And every one of them urged me not to be sad. They
insisted that they would find me another wife as caring and
beautiful as the deceased one.

"Now that my donkey has died, has any one of you offered me condolences, shared my grief, or suggested replac-
ing my donkey who has been my constant helper and friend
over the years?"

When his donkey was young and playful, it would leap
and romp mischievously. In one of its teasing moods, it ran
around in circles, finally bounded off across the fields, and
disappeared. Djuha looked for it everywhere on his farm,
in the vegetable garden, in the barn, in the stable, in the
cornfield. He inquired of all his neighbors. The animal was
nowhere to be found.

To everybody's surprise, Djuha remained calm. He did
not seem devastated or even saddened by his loss. Instead,
the neighbors assisting him in the search heard him whisper under his breath, "Thank you, O Allah, creator of all

living beings, for your kind consideration of your servant Djuha!"

One of the villagers was curious and inquired, "Djuha, it is hard for me to understand your attitude. I would have expected you to be devastated at the loss of your donkey. Yet you stand there reciting prayers of gratitude to Allah. Tell us, Djuha, how come?"

"The answer is simple," responded Djuha. "I am thanking all-powerful Allah for my good fortune. Don't you realize how lucky it was that my donkey was alone when it was lost? Had we been together as is customary, I would have gone astray with it and then I would have been lost as well. How then would I have searched for my beloved donkey until I found it?"

All of the affection and interdependence Djuha and his donkey had for each other came into play when Djuha's neighbor arrived one day and asked, "I have a favor to ask of you. Will you be kind enough to lend me your donkey?"

You can imagine how Djuha felt. His neighbor was asking for his means of transportation, his partner in work, his access to recreation, to friendship and love. And yet the Good Book states clearly you must love your neighbor and treat him as you would have him treat you!

What was Djuha to do? Instinctively, he resorted to subterfuge. Before he could think matters through, he heard himself say spontaneously, "Dear neighbor, I would like to be of service to you, as I value your friendship. However, it happens that my donkey is not at home today. My son required his help and has him for a day or . . ."

He had hardly finished when the donkey, chafing at its incarceration in the stable, started to bray at the top of its hee-hawing power.

The neighbor smiled and when he could be heard above the braying, offered the comment, "It seems I am blessed with good luck, and your donkey is at home with you today. It would appear that you can lend him to me after all."

"What!" exclaimed Djuha in anger. "Do you accept the word of my donkey, and doubt me, your friend for many years, old and true, with beard as white as the sand in the sun?"

On another occasion, a neighbor arrived in a terrible hurry. "Djuha," he gasped breathlessly, "please, Djuha let me borrow your donkey for an hour or two, to get something in town for my wife. She's in our kitchen baking a cake, and she suddenly finds that she has no almonds and honey, two absolutely necessary ingredients."

Djuha's surprising response was that he would have to consult the donkey, as he would not force it to do anything against its will. And off he went to the stable for the consultation, presumably to get the animal's consent.

After a while he returned, and said solemnly, "As I told you, I have discussed your request with my donkey. It refuses to go with you. When I tried to use persuasion, it convinced me of the correctness of its original decision."

In a rage, the neighbor shouted, "What do you mean, the animal convinced you! What did it say to you?"

"It refuses to accompany you," replied Djuha, "because of your behavior last time you borrowed it. It insists that you beat and cursed it. The faithful animal also refuses to listen to you once again, as you many times before cursed its owner, Djuha, who has been such a good friend to you."

Djuha had done many things to earn a living. Once between jobs, he thought of how many people love sour pickles and decided to become a hawker of pickles from his wagon drawn by his donkey.

He waited until he and his wife, Zahida, had grown a sufficient crop of crisp, fresh cucumbers. Zahida marinated them in vinegar and sugar steeped in garlic and other spices. When they were perfectly vinegrated, he bottled them and loaded them carefully in baskets on his donkey's back.

Leading the animal carefully through the narrow streets

of his town, he called out as loudly as he could, "Pickles! Sour pickles! Who wants crisp, sour pickles?"

Every time the donkey heard the word "pickles," it started to bray as loudly as it could, competing with Djuha at his own game. The donkey seemed to win; it brayed deafeningly and no one could hear its master.

This irritated Djuha so much that he might have beaten the animal if he were not so fond of it. Instead, he turned around and confronted the ass, shouting at it furiously, "Look here! Who's selling these pickles, you or I?"

Once when Djuha was shopping in town, he bought a large sack of dried beans and another sack of hayseed and placed them in the two colorful pockets of his donkey's handwoven saddlebag. Then he raised the saddlebag above his head and placed it across his own shoulders. He mounted the donkey and set out on the road leading to his village.

On the way home, he saw his neighbor Ibrahim coming toward him. "*Al salaam aleikem!*" he called out in a warm singsong.

"*Aleikem salaam!*" returned the villager, who stopped and stared at him in amazement.

"Why are you looking at me like that?" asked Djuha. "Is there something wrong?"

"Djuha," replied Ibrahim, "forgive me, but why are you carrying on your own shoulders a heavy saddlebag with two full pockets? Why don't you do as others do, and place the saddlebag on your donkey's back instead?"

"Inconsiderate man!" shouted Djuha. "Don't you fear the retribution of Allah? Aren't we supposed to be kind to animals? Isn't it enough that this poor animal, on whose many kindnesses I depend, has to carry me? Do you also want it to carry the saddlebag filled with two heavy sacks?"

This last donkey story is not about Djuha's favorite animal, but about the Sultan and his pet white donkey on whom the ruler lavished much love and affection. He admired his donkey so much that he became very unhappy because the animal could not speak to him.

So intelligent was the white donkey and so lovable as a companion, that the Sultan became convinced it could develop language if properly taught. He searched up and down his kingdom for a gifted teacher who would assume the task of instructing this charming animal in the art of language. Despite his offer of a generous reward, no one volunteered to undertake the assignment.

When Djuha heard about this unique opportunity, he appeared before the Sultan and in his most self-assured manner proclaimed, "Your Highness, I have a donkey with which I communicate constantly, but I am acquainted with it many years. I will teach your beautiful donkey the same skill if you grant me sufficient time and certain conditions."

The ruler was delighted. "I am ready to grant any reasonable request if in the end you will return my donkey with the gift of speech."

"First of all," said Djuha, "you must grant me ten years at least for the teaching period. For the duration of my instruction I will need a house large enough for me and my family, several servants, a stable, and a stable boy who will care for your white donkey in the style to which it is accustomed. There must, of course, be food for my family and for all the helpers. Only under these conditions will I be able to devote myself exclusively to this project, which will demand all my time and energy."

The Sultan, delighted at the offer, gave Djuha a house, servants, and plenty of money to satisfy all his needs. Finally, he reminded Djuha of the law which required that he fulfill his agreement or else receive the mandatory punishment of beheading without mercy.

For the next few years Djuha lived in more luxury than he had ever known. He was enjoying his easy life when a group of his friends visited him and reminded him of the consequences of his arrangement with the Sultan.

"Djuha," they said, "what dangerous and foolish journey have you embarked on? You know very well that you cannot succeed in teaching the Sultan's donkey to speak! How are you going to escape the penalty of beheading, which is certain to be your fate?"

Djuha listened to them calmly and reassured them. "I am grateful to all of you for your affection and expression of concern," he said, "but I am in little danger of receiving the ultimate penalty.

"Why should I worry? During the ten years of my contract with the Sultan, one of three things may happen: the Sultan may die, or I may die, though I am younger than he, or the donkey may die, and he has a shorter life expectancy than either of us.

"And with Allah's great power, who knows, the donkey may even learn to speak," he added, with a solemn look on his face and a twinkle in his eye.

I hope these anecdotes about Djuha and his donkey give you a glimpse at the importance of the donkey in the life of the *fellah*. It is not the "ass" or dumb animal you will find in some folktales, but the companion and helper of man in his work on the farm. Most of all, it is an object of love, gratitude, humor, and fun.

# 31

# DJUHA BORROWS A POT
## Arab Version

Djuha had enough small pots to cook meals for his family, but he did not have a very large roasting pan. That presented a real problem when he decided to make a gala party to celebrate the birth of his youngest grandchild. He was determined to roast a whole lamb with a delicious stuffing and to invite all his friends.

And Djuha had many friends. He knew everybody in his village and many people in the city of Damascus, as well as in the surrounding countryside. As he traveled around, he kept inviting more and more people, until he became aware that he would need a large lamb and a humongous pot.

The problem of procuring a lamb would be easy to solve: he would slaughter one of his own flock. But he would have to borrow a cauldron. He finally located one that he could borrow for the occasion; it was owned by a friend of a friend, the proprietor of a restaurant in the Damascus bazaar.

When the week of the celebration approached, Djuha drove his *arabana*, or wagon pulled by a mule, to the Damascus bazaar and tied it to a stanchion at the entrance. From the back of his *arabana*, he rolled his wheelbarrow down to the street.

He pushed it through the narrow cobblestoned alleys of the bazaar, past dresses waving in the wind, red velvet with gold metallic embroidery, turquoise velvet with silver metallic embroidery; past shops with silver jewelry, necklaces, brooches, earrings, and bracelets all set with coral, turquoise, or well-cut carnelian; past shops with decorative copper and brass urns, coffeepots, and small copper bowls of great beauty; past cafes where people sat leisurely smoking narghiles or sipping tea and coffee and eating sweet honey cakes and delicious *zlabiah* and halvah.

When he came to the restaurant, he rolled his three-cornerd wheelbarrow to the back door leading to the kitchen, where the restaurateur greeted him, "*Al salaam aleikem!*"

"*Aleikem salaam!*" responded Djuha. "As you promised, I've come to borrow the large cauldron that will enable me to serve roasted lamb fit for a king to celebrate the birth of my youngest grandchild. May Allah bless you for your generosity!"

He lifted the pot onto the wheelbarrow and pushed the whole heavy burden, the wheels rattling over cobblestones and the pot clanging against its cover, until he arrived at his wagon, which he loaded for the trip home. His faithful mule brought him to the village on the outskirts of Damascus where he lived.

On the day of the party, wonderful odors emanated from Djuha's kitchen, as the mouthwatering lamb stuffed with rice, chopped meat, sharia, and parsley was roasted in onions and garlic. The food was delicious: salads of humus, tahini, tabbouleh, baba ghanoush, and on top of it all, a dessert of baklava dripping with honey.

When it was all eaten and everybody was sated, Djuha made sure that the large copper pot was scoured inside and polished outside. Then he took the trip back to Damascus, through the narrow streets of the bazaar, to the back kitchen door of the restaurant, and returned the shiny pot.

As the restaurateur was thanking Djuha for the prompt restitution, he noticed a small pot, an exact replica of the larger one, nested in it. "What is this?" he asked in surprise, as he took the miniature pot out of the larger one and looked at it admiringly.

"Oh," said Djuha with a smile, "I forgot to tell you that

while your big pot was in my house, it gave birth to a small one exactly in its own image. Congratulations and Allah's blessings on your house!"

The restaurateur was incredulous, yet delighted. "May Allah bless you, too, with such births," he said graciously, and took the two pots into his kitchen.

Djuha made his way back through the bazaar, past shops with huge many-colored rugs; past shops with bridal dresses and ornate jewelry for rent or for sale; past shops full of furniture made of black wood with ivory inlaid mosaic; past shops where silver objects both religious and secular were sold, and copper and brass objects shone out in the relative darkness of the bazaar.

When he arrived home, he washed his mule down, fed it, and felt that he had accomplished what he needed to that day.

A few weeks later, Djuha returned to the bazaar again. He was about to make another huge party to celebrate the wedding of his oldest granddaughter. Again he needed to borrow the huge cauldron to cook for the many guests he was expecting.

The restaurateur wished Djuha's family well. "May Allah grant your lovely young granddaughter great happiness and many children from a joyous marriage!"

He then walked back to his kitchen and told the cook to prepare the cauldron, wondering how Djuha would surprise him this time. With the pot in his wheelbarrow, Djuha wended his way back through the narrow cobblestoned streets.

Days and then weeks passed, and Djuha did not return with the cauldron. Finally, the restaurateur decided to visit Djuha and find out for himself what was delaying the return of his property.

When he arrived at Djuha's home, he exchanged the usual pleasantries, then discreetly asked about the large pot he had lent Djuha for use at his granddaughter's wedding.

"Haven't you heard, my friend?" responded Djuha, his face darkening with sadness. "Perhaps I should have returned to your restaurant in the bazaar to tell you. I am truly sorry, but while it was in my house, your unfortunate cauldron died and I had to bury it. I was certain that the sad news had reached you."

"What do you mean!" shouted the restaurateur. "My pot died? Since when can a copper pot die?"

"Surely," responded Djuha, shaking his head thoughtfully, "if a cauldron can give birth, it can also die."

Just as thoughtfully, the restaurateur turned around and walked back to the kitchen, where his cook would have one less pot than he had before this story began.

# 32

# THE BEETLE
# WHO WISHED
# TO GET MARRIED

There was a black beetle who wanted to marry.
She liked the idea and didn't wish to tarry.
She cleaned the yard
And earned a piaster
She scrubbed the porch
And earned a piaster
She swept the room
And earned a piaster.

She went to the souk and bought powder and
   paint.
She added antimony to make her look quaint.
Reddened her cheeks,
Powdered her nose,
Blackend her brows,
Colored her lips,
Darkened her lashes,
And looked proudly in the mirror.

Then she stood by her tiny wee house, at the
   door,
A peddler of sweets passed with halvah galore.
He saw her standing there
And asked, "Why're you here?

Why do you stand
By your house?
What do you seek
At your own front door?"

The little black beetle told the truth to the peddler:
She wished a kind husband to love, not a meddler.
"I'll take you to wife,"
Said the peddler.

The beetle then asked,
"And after our marriage,
With what will you beat me?"
Said the sweets seller,
"With my halvah tray—hard!"

Said the little black beetle, "Go away, go away!
I'll not marry you, I don't like what you say.
For I can clean house,
I can make salads,
And I grill kabob,
My coffee smells good,
I can even sell halvah,
And I can bear children."

The little black beetle turned her face from this
    seller.
Came another: "Radishes! Radishes!" He sure
    was a bellower.
The little black beetle told the truth to this peddler:
She wanted a good husband to love, not a meddler.
"I'll take you to wife,"
Said the peddler.

The beetle then asked,
"And after our marriage,
With what will you beat me?"
Said the radish seller,
"With my radish roots—hard!"

Said the little black beetle, "Go away, go away!
I'll not marry you; I don't like what you say,
For I can clean house,
I can make salads,
And I grill kabob,
My coffee smells good,
I can even sell radishes,
And I can bear children."

The little black beetle turned her face from this seller.
Another came by. "Onions! Seed-giving
     onions!" A bellower.
The little black beetle told the truth to this
     peddler:
She wished a kind husband to love, not a
     meddler.
"I'll take you to wife,"
Said the peddler.

The beetle then asked,
"And after our marriage,
With what will you beat me?"
Said the onion seller,
"With an onion—hard!"

Said the little black beetle, "Go away, go away!
I'll not marry you; I don't like what you say!
For I can clean house,
I can make salads,
And I grill kabob,
My coffee smells good,
I can even sell onions,
And I can bear children."

The little black beetle turned her face from this seller.
Came another: "Pickles for sale! Sour pickles!" A bellower.
The little black beetle told the truth to this
     peddler:

She wished a kind husband to love, not a
     meddler.
"I'll take you to wife,"
Said the peddler.

The beetle then asked,
"And after our marriage,
With what will you beat me?"
Said the pickle merchant,
"With this jar of pickles—hard!"

Said the little black beetle, "Go away, Go away!
I'll not marry you; I don't like what you say!
For I can clean house,
I can make salads,
And I grill kabob,
My coffee smells good,
I can even sell pickles,
And I can bear children."

The beetle once more stood by the door of her tiny
     wee house.
Then came, with nothing to sell, no bellow or
     shout, a mouse,
Who asked in a teeny wee voice that befitted a
     mouse,
"Why do you stand by the door of your house?"

The little black beetle told the truth to the mouse:
She wanted to marry and needed a spouse.
"I'll take you to wife,"
Said the wee little mouse.

The beetle then asked,
"And after our marriage,
With what will you beat me?"
Said the mouse,
"With my tail, g-e-n-t-l-y."

Said the beetle, "You may stay, please do stay.
For you I will marry; I like what you say!
For you I'll clean house,
For you I'll make salads,
For you I'll grill kabob,
And my coffee smells good,
I'll even help you work,
And I can bear children."

The wedding lasted seven days and seven nights;
Their guests were the beetles and lizards and
    mice
Who danced and cavorted and gave good advice:
The bride and the groom performed all of the
    rites.
She forgot about halvah, onion, radish, and
    pickle,
For the mouse was her husband, she'd never be
    fickle!

# 33

# THREE SISTERS,
# THE PRINCE,
# AND THE MAGIC POT

Once upon a time, there were three sisters who lived together in a small hut at the edge of an old city. All three earned their bread by spinning flax into thread. And all were as beautiful as the full moon in a clear autumn sky.

However, while Yasmeen, the youngest, was kind-hearted, generous, and charming, the elder sisters were mean and spiteful. It was not surprising that they eventually became jealous of Yasmeen's disposition that endeared her to people.

One day, after weaving for several hours, Yasmeen looked at the many spools of fine thread she had amassed. Satisfied with the quality of her product, she decided to go to the *souk* to sell it. She was delighted when the first cloth weaver she approached liked her thread and bought the whole lot for a good price.

With time on her hands, she sauntered among the crowded stalls in which brass and copper pots vied for her attention with colorful woven fabrics and garments. Suddenly, her eyes rested on a lovely ceramic pot with a colorful blue and yellow design. She bought it and took it, loosely wrapped in an old newspaper, to her room at the edge of the city.

She placed it carefully on a low table in her bedroom. After filling it with water, she slipped a red rose into it and sat down to enjoy its beauty.

"Isn't it pretty?" she asked her sisters, who had followed her to see what she had in the paper she was carrying.

"No, I think it's ugly!" snapped the eldest.

"And a shocking waste of money!" added the middle sister.

Then off they went to the market to peddle their thread.

Yasmeen lifted the little pot in both hands and stroked it lovingly.

"How beautiful it is!" she said to herself. "How I wish I had a dress as beautiful as this little pot!"

To her amazement, a silken robe floated down from the air and unseen hands laid it across her knees.

"Oh!" she gasped. "This must be a magic pot, like Aladdin's lamp!"

She picked up the dress and unfolded it gently. She gasped with delight, for it was made of the finest pale blue silk, and trimmed with sapphires and diamonds. It was lovelier than any garment she had ever seen when window-shopping in the fine shop section of the bazaar. Was the wonderful gown made for royalty and would it disappear when she awoke from this dream?

After pinching herself to make sure she was truly awake, she took off her plain brown cotton frock and put on her new dress. Then she walked about the room, looking at herself in the mirror, loving the soft feel of the silk , the faint rustle of its folds, and the iridescent blue that brought out the warmth of her skin color. She was astonished at her own lovely image. The room seemed full of sunshine, and she was radiant in her happiness.

Suddenly, she stopped short. "I'm hungry," she murmured to herself. "I wonder if the magic pot would give me something to eat."

She cupped it in her hands and whispered to it, afraid to be too bold, "Little pot, little pot, I wish I had something good to eat."

The unseen hands covered her table with a fine cloth of embroidered linen and set down a large silver dish of delicious skewered shish kebab, small dishes containing salads of couscous, humus, green peppers, and tomatoes, a selection of sweet tarts, honey cakes, jellies, and a jug of iced sherbet. She had never had a more delicious meal.

She was finishing the sweetmeats when she heard her sisters at the door. Quickly she wished away the tablecloth and everything on it, as well as the blue silk dress. When her sisters entered the house Yasmeen was busy at her spinning wheel.

In the days that followed her good fortune at the bazaar, she did not dare tell them about the magic pot; she was certain they would take it away from her. When they left the house or were fast asleep in their beds, she wished for dresses, jewels, flowers, and delicious food, as well as many other wonderful things. Then she wished them away again—except for the food, which she had already eaten.

One day shortly after she had acquired her magic pot, she went to the *souk* as usual to sell her spools of woven thread. Suddenly, she heard the blast of trumpets signaling an important announcement from the palace.

Then a great voice boomed, "Listen all ye citizens of Basra! Happiness has descended upon our Sultan's family! Prince Yusuf, son of our beloved Sultan, will reach his twenty-first birthday next month, and our joyous royal family invites all the citizens of our great city to join in the celebration. Hear ye! You are all invited to a festive feast on the seventh day of *Ramadan!*"

Yasmeen's heart jumped into her throat. She thought of the beautiful dress, cloak, and jewels she could wear to such a celebration, just by rubbing her magic pot. But she knew in her heart that her sisters would not permit her to go.

And so it was. When the night of the feast came, the elder sisters put on their best clothes and went off to the palace. They had informed her that she must stay at home to look after the house.

Left alone, Yasmeen went to her room and lovingly caressed her pot. "Magic pot, little magic pot, I do wish with all my heart to go to the Sultan's feast tonight and to be the fairest among all the maidens. I wish for the most beautiful gown and robe and jewels in the world!"

In the blink of an eye, the unseen hands laid clothes gently across her bed and heaped magnificent jewels on her table. Eagerly she changed into the long dress of glistening soft green silk, a red waistcoat and mantle, and an embroidered green veil that covered her face up to her eyes, according to the custom. All the garments were made of the most delicate silk the silkworms of China had ever spun.

She slipped her little feet into silver shoes, and finally selected jewels from the vast array of emeralds, pearls, and diamonds piled before her. She braided her hair with a long string of little diamonds and emeralds that glistened and danced in the light. On her neck she clasped a glorious diamond necklace, and on both her small wrists and her equally slender ankles she fastened golden bracelets set with diamonds and emeralds.

When Yasmeen looked in her mirror, she had hopes that she would indeed be the fairest of the fair. She then joined the long line of citizens headed for the palace.

Once there, she was ushered into the Queen's apartment with all the other women, for men and women were kept separate, as was the custom. She was disappointed that she would not see the Prince, but felt comfortable enough to lower her veil in the presence of girls and women. She looked so different from her usual self in the everyday brown cotton dress that no one recognized her, not even her sisters.

So struck was the group by her beauty, charm, and modesty, that they gathered around her admiringly, wondering who she was. The Queen invited her to sit at the royal table. Yasmeen had never before known such happiness.

Nevertheless, she was troubled. How was she to get home

before her sisters and avoid their terrible anger? They might even beat her, as they had several times before.

When the feast was ended, the entertainment began, and the young palace maidens stood up to sing and dance. While the Queen and her guests focused their attention on the dancers, Yasmeen slipped away quietly.

Confused by the intricate maze of the palace, she lost her way and found herself in the stable yard. In the darkness she caught her foot in a horse trough, losing one of her anklets. She did not dare stop to look for it, but hurried home. When her two sisters arrived, she was in her coarse brown dress, working at her spinning wheel.

Early the next day, Prince Yusuf entered the stable to mount his favorite horse for his customary morning ride. He found his grooms trying to control his horse, which reared up when led to the trough. His usually calm steed balked, snorted, and stamped, and refused to drink.

The Prince approached the horse trough. There, glistening under the water, was a small shiny object. He reached for it and was astonished to find an ornate anklet of gold, set with what appeared to be diamonds and emeralds. A strange feeling shot through his entire body, starting from his fingertips, which tingled from the touch of the beautiful anklet.

He rushed to his father's quarters.

"My lord and father!" he said, trying to control his excitement. "Yesterday you encouraged me to find a bride among the guests at my birthday feast. I had no desire then to marry because I had never met a maiden who attracted me. Now by a turn of fate, I believe I have changed my mind."

He told the strange story of the anklet to the Sultan. "I feel a certain closeness with the maiden who wore this! Surely she must be beautiful with so slim an ankle."

The Sultan's response was immediate. "She must certainly be the daughter of a rich lord!" He smiled in amusement.

"I will marry her!" cried the Prince impetuously.

"Well, as to that, my son," said the Sultan, "go to your mother the Queen and talk to her. She is the expert in matters of the heart."

Yusuf rushed off to the Queen, who recognized the anklet at once.

"Yusuf," she said, looking deeply into his eyes, "through this anklet you may be able to identify a most attractive young woman who came to the feast last night. No one knew her, but we all admired her beauty, modesty, and charm. For some strange reason, she disappeared before I could ask her who she was and where she had come from."

"O my lady and my mother," urged the Prince, "I beg you to find her for me. She has taken hold of my heart, although I have never even seen her. And I will love no other!"

The Queen, who had herself had as strong a reaction to Yasmeen, was delighted at her son's words, although she wondered at his impetuous judgment of the girl by the size of her ankle. She nevertheless immediately sent her herald out to search throughout the city for the beautiful young woman who had worn the anklet at the feast.

As you would expect, the herald started his search in the houses of the great lords and rich merchants. To his amazement, none of their daughters had ankles slim enough. He continued on toward the edge of the city until he came upon the three sisters' small hut.

"The anklet is mine," Yasmeen said as soon as she understood the herald's mission. She slipped the lovely anklet on. Astonished, her sisters looked on in silence.

The herald bowed to her. "Fair maiden, you are summoned by the Queen and I am to lead you to her immediately."

"Grant me a moment to get ready," answered Yasmeen.

She disappeared into her room, caressed her blue and yellow pot, and wished for the green dress and veil, the red jerkin and robe, and the other golden anklet. She came out dressed as she had been at the feast the night before and joined the herald, leaving her sisters so amazed that they could not find words, not even to try to stop her.

Yasmeen entered the Queen's chamber, knelt, and bowed her forehead to the ground. The Queen graciously raised her up, embraced her, and murmured, "My sweet child, I am happy to see you again."

She sent one of her attendants to fetch her son Yusuf, who came in great haste, eager to meet the young woman who, sight unseen, had aroused so much feeling in him.

With the two young people standing before her, the Queen granted Yasmeen permission to remove her veil. Obeying her monarch, the young woman blushed as she appeared unveiled before a young man for the first time. The two stood gazing at each other in embarrassment and delight, for neither one had ever before had such amazingly deep feelings of attraction for another human being.

You may be sure that the marriage date was set immediately and a lavish celebration planned for the whole community. But this is not your typical Cinderella story. For these two young people had to endure profound suffering before they could live happily ever after.

While the preparations for the wedding were going on at the palace, Yasmeen, with her usual generosity, decided to provide her sisters with clothes as beautiful as her own. And that is how they found out the secret of the little magic pot.

Her sisters, while pretending to he happy for her, were filled with burning jealousy. They planned to prevent the marriage no matter at what cost to their sister's happiness. Finally, they concocted an evil plot.

One day, while Yasmeen was out, they sneaked into her room and rubbed the little pot, asking it to give them a magic pin with which they could accomplish their wicked scheme. Then they waited for the wedding day with glee, so sure were they that they would succeed in their malevolent plot.

The day dawned in a glorious display of color as if nature itself rejoiced at the happiness of Yasmeen and Yusuf.

The preparations at the palace were completed; wonderful odors of food and flowers competed with each other throughout the palace grounds.

The two sisters, in a false show of affection for the young bride, helped her into her white gossamer dress. Then, while they were brushing her hair, they pushed the magic pin into her head as far as it would go. She immediately changed from a lovely, happy woman to a small soft-feathered white dove. They stumbled over each other in their efforts to catch the bird so that they might complete their evil plan, but she flew out the window and disappeared from view.

Weeping and tearing their hair as if in grief, the two wicked sisters ran to the palace and interrupted the happy Prince in his preparation for the evening's festivities. Sobbing, they told the prince that Yasmeen had left the house some hours before and had not returned. No one had seen where she went and, although they had looked everywhere, they could not find her.

"Our dear, dear sister," they moaned. "Our dear little sister was so happy and now she has disappeared! What shall we do? What shall we do?"

The Sultan's guards and the Queen's attendants searched everywhere. They panned throughout the bazaars and entered every house for miles around. They entered the forest and the fields and the caves in the area. Yasmeen was nowhere to be found, nor was there any trace of her.

Prince Yusuf, heartbroken, lay in his chamber, receiving nothing but bad news every day, unable to eat or sleep in his misery. The only thing that cheered him was the presence of a beautiful white dove perched on his windowsill, cooing softly.

One day he opened the window and the dove flew into his room. He held out his finger toward her, and she perched on it, rubbing her head lovingly against his chest. Surprised and delighted with the gentle creature, he stroked her head gently. Suddenly, he felt something hard among the feathers on her head.

"What is this in your head, little dove?" he murmured softly, cooing back to her.

She responded in soft cooing tones. Then she turned her head so that he could see the hard object more clearly. When he parted her feathers, he saw the large head of a pin. He pulled at it. It came out in his hand, and in a moment his beautiful bride stood before him in her white gossamer wedding dress.

You can just imagine their happiness and the joy of everybody from the Sultan and his Queen to all of their people except for two—the wicked sisters. What happened to them? You wish to know, don't you? Well, they were so angry, frustrated, and frightened that they swooned and died.

Prince Yusuf and Princess Yasmeen did live happily ever after. The magic pot gave them everything they needed, and Allah blessed them with many beautiful children.

# 34

# A CONTEST IN SIGN LANGUAGE
## Arab Version

Many years ago, in the days before trains, automobiles, and airplanes, travel was slow and tedious. The distance between Iran and Egypt seemed as great then as the distance between the earth and the moon does today. When scholars from Ispahan came to Cairo by camel and sailboat, their reputations were accepted in Egypt without question, since confirmation would be a lengthy process.

You can imagine the furor in Cairo when a Persian scholar arrived and declared that he was the most learned vizier in his own land and the greatest scholar in the world in sign language. His purpose was to pit his wisdom against all the wise men of the royal court of Egypt.

The King of Egypt, hospitable and respectful of learning, appointed the Iranian scholar to a high position at court. Egyptian professors, however, were skeptical of the world-wide reputation he claimed to have. They wondered why he had been positioned above them in their own country.

Some great scholars at Al Azhar, the Golden University of Islam in Cairo, asked their King for an audience.

When they stood before him, they pleaded, "O Great King, Messenger of Allah on Earth and Jewel of the World, hear our cause. You have elevated this foreigner above us in the scholarly circles of Cairo, and we feel demeaned. Grant us the opportunity of testing his scholarship against our own.

"Let the Iranian ask us as profound a series of questions as he wishes, and if our responses do not reflect equal scholarship with his, we stand ready to acknowledge him our superior in learning. If he cannot defeat us in this contest, we request that he be sent back to his own country. And you will judge the depth of his questions and the quality of our responses."

The King accepted their challenge as fair to both the foreign scholar and to his counterparts in Egypt. The monarch agreed to be the judge at the contest. He immediately ordered his nobles, the scholars, and all the attendants at the court to convene in his audience hall.

When the entire court and the faculty of the university were assembled, all the cleverest men in the land were there. At a signal from the King, the Persian sage from Ispahan rose and, without a word, made a gesture toward the Egyptian scholars. He waited for a response from them. When none was forthcoming, he announced in a loud voice:

"Though this gesture of mine was profound,
Its purpose was not to confound;
If you've mastered logic and divinity,
Interpret correctly and mock me with impunity.
If your scholarship is deficient
Or your reasoning inefficient,
You'll admit you made a big gaffe,
And together we'll have a good laugh."

Not one of the brilliant scholars of Cairo had a clue to the meaning of the Iranian's gesture. Rather than concede the contest, they maintained their good humor and one of them responded in rhyme:

"We do respect your great learning;
For a correct solution we're yearning.
Give us six long days to cogitate:
We'll then be ready to pontificate."

The King granted his scholars a six-day cogitation period. They were to spend the time thinking and to come up with the key to the Persian's sign, as well as a way to respond to it in the same sign language.

The scholars spent many hours in libraries and cafes discussing the apparently unfathomable sign language. How were they to find a way to compete successfully with the Persian so that he would go back to his country and cease intruding on their scholarliness?

Although their tongues wagged and their beards bobbed up and down, they found no solution to their dilemma.

Then Suliman, one of the wisest among them, offered a suggestion: "Perhaps we are too clever to decipher this conundrum. As you know, young children in their innocence often find solutions to problems that confound their parents. Let us try to find a totally uneducated peasant who, in his ignorance will stumble on the key to the Persian's sign language."

Because of his excellent proposal and since his was the only one, he was appointed to find a naive person, ignorant of the complicated thought processes of scholars.

Off he went to the bazaar, where peasants often crouched with a vegetable or two for sale in order to keep body and soul together. Sure enough, he came upon a young man with the soil still in his fingernails, who had one egg and a few carrots to sell. Suliman grabbed him by the shoulder, saying, "Come with me, my son, I want to talk with you."

The poor peasant was frightened. He did not know what to expect on his first visit to a big city. Thoughts raced through his head one after the other: "Should I go with him? Does he want to steal my carrots and egg? Maybe I'd better hide my produce in my shirt and make a run for it!"

But Suliman held him fast, and seeing that the lad was frightened, tried to calm him down by asking him in a friendly tone, "What is your name, my son?"

"Abdulla, O great Sheikh," was the response given in a

voice shaking with fear. The boy pulled away as if to break for it and run. What was he doing in conversation with a wise and knowledgeable long-bearded Sheikh of Al Azhar?

"Don't be afraid, Abdulla," soothed the scholar. "I want to benefit you, not harm you.

"Come with me and meet a Persian gentleman who talks only in signs and gestures, not words. He has challenged all of us in Cairo to converse with him in his peculiar way, without speech. I want you to watch him, get his meaning, and reply to him by signs, not words, because that is his language. Abdulla, if you can do this, you will be richer by a handful of piasters."

The youth kissed the scholar's hand in gratitude. "May Allah watch over you and may you have a long life, kind sir! My family is very poor and my mother is sick. I need money to take her to the doctor. My few carrots and my egg will spoil if I don't sell them soon, and the market is very slow today."

"Good boy!" said the scholar. "Come with me and meet many sheikhs and scholars who have not been able to converse with the Persian in his sign language. See if you can do better than they."

The others were shocked when they saw Suliman's choice, a *fellah* with grimy face, matted hair, patched clothes, and hands encrusted with the soil in which he toiled. However, they had no alternative but to go ahead with their plan.

They gave Abdulla and his peasant shirt a thorough washing and dressed him in an abaya, or long cloak, with black and tan stripes. They shampooed and combed his disheveled hair and covered it with a white *kaffiyeh* embroidered in black, topped by a shiny black *agol* to hold it in place. For his feet, he was given a pair of new leather slippers.

He was transformed. The scholars led him to the King's audience hall to do battle with the Persian in the presence of His Majesty himself and a large circle of amirs, viziers, and court attendants. Abdulla, afraid he might lose his carrots and egg or have them stolen, held them close to his body inside his rough hair inner shirt.

The King sat on his throne in the center of the circle of courtiers and scholars. The Persian sat on one side of the inner circle, adjusting his turban, the peasant on the other, looking calm and comfortable.

The King's attendants beat upon the royal gongs. The hall became totally silent except for the audible breathing of the expectant crowd. "In the name of Allah the Merciful let the contest begin!" the King's voice resounded throughout the hall.

At a signal from the monarch, the Persian scholar arose from his cushion and pointed one finger at Abdulla. To everybody's surprise the peasant did not hesitate, but immediately pointed two fingers aggressively at the foreigner.

The courtiers, totally engrossed in this strange scene, saw the look of astonishment on the Persian's face and watched him closely as he continued. The scholar raised his hand toward the ceiling and held it there. Again, without hesitation, the peasant placed his hand flat on the floor.

The King, the Egyptian scholars, and the courtiers observed the Persian's surprised look, as he continued the contest. He reached into a large box that he had carried into the hall, and to everybody's amazement, pulled out a live hen and threw it at the peasant. What did Abdulla do? He reached into his shirt and pulled out his egg, which he deliberately threw at the scholar.

The Persian rose and in a loud voice spoke for the first time since the contest had begun:

"Your Sheikh has proven his depth of knowledge;
I've met my equal in contest, I will not hedge:
He has answered my signs with wisdom and
    clarity;
I return to Ispahan to declare Egyptian parity."

The Egyptian King and the scholars of Cairo rose in excitement. They congratulated the bewildered Abdulla, rewarding him with a large bagful of piasters that would pay for his mother's visit to the doctor and for food his family would enjoy for many moons.

The scholars, happy at the outcome, were nevertheless as ignorant of sign language and as mystified by the contest as they had been at the very outset. What was the meaning of the Persian's signs and of the peasant's responses?

The scholar Suliman did not return to the *souk* with his companions, as he could not endure remaining ignorant of this strange method of communication. What did the Iranian scholar sign that could be understood by the Egyptian *fellah*? And what did the peasant answer to impress the Persian with the depth of his knowledge? He decided to find out.

He put his arm around Abdulla's shoulders and walked with him, congratulating him on his performance. "You did very well, young man, and we are all proud of you. But tell me, what did the Persian's gestures mean? How did you understand him and know what to respond?"

"Well," said Abdulla simply, "when the learned gentleman pointed his finger at my eye, I understood his meaning to be, 'If you don't keep your eye open, I'll poke my finger into it, like this.'

"I don't like to be threatened, and I got angry. So I got back at him by pointing fingers at both his eyes, warning him that if he got funny with me I'd give him what for. I'd poke out both his eyes, not one.

"Then when he held his hand up for quite a long while, I thought he was threatening me again. I understood him to say that if I attacked him, he would hang me from the rafters. I wouldn't take that, so I showed him by pressing my hand on the floor that I could throw him down and easily bash his brains in.

"That upset him, so he decided to get the better of me by boasting that he always ate the finest chicken, and he threw one at me to prove his point. Well, I couldn't take that, could I? It was lucky that I had my egg hidden underneath my shirt, so I took it out and threw it at him to show him that I eat just as well as he does.

"You heard what he said after that. He praised my wisdom and said he would go home. Isn't that what you wanted? It must have been, because the King gave me a bagful of piasters, and you hugged me and congratulated me."

Suliman listened to this explanation in great astonishment and assured Abdulla again that he had done well.

When he heard that the Persian was joining the next caravan from Cairo to Ispahan, Suliman decided to see him off and hear his side of the story.

He joined the scholar at the khan caravansary, and said, "O knowledgeable Persian, may Allah provide a safe journey and a happy reunion with your family in Ispahan! But tell me before you leave us, how it was that our young friend was able to understand your sign language although he had never experienced it before? How did he respond to you so well that you understood his untutored communication? Did you comprehend his gestures, and what meaning did you get from them?"

"Your young man was very clever and carefully taught," answered the Persian scholar. "I have tried to have this dispute with scholars in many countries, and never before have I found one who understood the challenges and responded to them with the depth of thought and knowledge shown by this young student of yours."

Suliman persisted. "Please tell me what your questions meant and what his responses were, so that I may learn from you and from the young student."

"This is the explanation, O learned Sheikh," responded the scholar from Ispahan. "You recall that I raised one finger toward him. I meant to say, 'There is no God but Allah, the only holy One.'

"Your young scholar responded immediately and correctly by raising two fingers toward me, showing he understood that Allah had a holy prophet, Mohammed, making two, not one.

"Then I raised my hand toward the roof and held it there for a few seconds. I meant to say, 'Allah supports the heavens without the need for pillars or beams.'

"Your profound scholar corrected me by putting his hand on the floor. He was pointing out that Allah is God of the earth as well as the sky, and needs no support for either.

"Then I threw my hen toward him to point out that Allah produces all living things from the inanimate. Your scholar was quick to show me his egg, indicating the truth that Allah also produces the inanimate from the living.

"So you see, I am full of admiration for Egyptian scholarship, since this was the first time in many years of engaging in this dispute all over the world that I have received thoughtful and valid responses to my challenges. Your young scholar must have an intelligent, as well as a well-tutored, mind! May Allah preserve him and all of his teachers in this wonderful city of Cairo!"

Suliman, the brilliant scholar of the Golden University of Al Azhar, bade farewell and a safe journey to the Persian scholar of Ispahan, and turned toward home. There he contemplated for many days the curious mystery of two people communicating with each other without mutual understanding and despite great differences in beliefs and education. Obviously, they could gesture and think they understood each other without meaning the same thing at all.

# 35

# TOTAL CONFUSION: WHY LEARN TO SPEAK?

I had always thought of speech as Allah's special gift to human beings, raising them above dumb animals. When I heard the story I am about to tell you, I began to entertain the idea that we would have done just as well without that gift. This is the story of three men without hearing and a dervish without speech.

I'll start with a stone-deaf goatherd who did very well guarding his flock and guiding them to places where grass for grazing pushed up between the stones in a rocky terrain. He had no need for hearing, since he, his goats, and his dogs communicated through their many kind acts and their affectionate behavior.

Even his wife and he got along well despite his deafness. Every morning she handed him a packet of food, to eat while the animals were nibbling away at the sparse grass of the harsh terrain. The grateful look in his eyes and the warm farewell hug she gave him were language they both understood.

One day, an unusual thing happened. He was on the other side of the mountain with his flock of goats chomping away at the tasty grass that pushed up between the stones. He reached into his backpack for his lunch, but for the first time ever, it was not there. It must still be on the kitchen table!

He figured out by the position of the sun in the sky that

it was past lunchtime. Yet his wife had not sent his meal with one of the children. He realized that she was not aware that he had left it. He would have to go home to get it, for how could he sit in the blazing heat for twelve hours without food and drink? But who would look after his flock while he was gone?

Luckily, there was a man cutting firewood on the upper part of the slope. Surely he would be of help.

The goatherd climbed up and spoke, "Peace be with you, my friend. I must return home to get my lunch, which I carelessly left behind this morning. Would you be kind enough to keep an eye on my goats? The dogs will see that they don't wander away. Would you just scare off any intruder who might try to steal one of my animals?"

Now, it just happened that the man chopping firewood was also deaf. Since he did not hear a word the goatherd had said, he responded, "No, I can't give you any of this wood for your home. I need some of it for my family and I sell the rest for my living!"

Then, waving his ax over his head, he continued, "Leave me alone! I have a lot more chopping to do!"

The goatherd assumed the stranger was waving him on and had agreed to look after the herd. "Thank you! Thank you for your kindness! Peace be with you!"

Off he ran toward his village. The woodcutter went back to his work.

When the goatherd returned with his lunch of bread, dates, cheese, and a container of water, his herd was grazing peacefully, and the woodcutter was still chopping wood. He counted the goats and was certain that all were safe and sound, except for one who had been lame for several days and appeared in great pain, limping badly.

Since the woodcutter had been so kind, he decided to make him a gift of the lame goat. "Goodness knows what would have happened to my goats if this kind woodcutter had not kept an eye on them," he said to himself. "There is nothing wrong with this goat except its lameness, and it really adds no value to my herd. When roasted it will provide this man's family with several tasty meals."

He lifted the goat to the back of his neck, holding its four feet in front of him. "My friend," he spoke out, "I want to reward you for guarding my flock while I returned home for my lunch today. Please accept this fine young animal. Despite its lame leg, it will provide you with a feast for your whole family."

The deaf woodcutter looked up at the goatherd with the lame goat on his back. Assuming that the man was accusing him of causing the injury, he shouted, "Why blame me for your animal's accident? I had nothing to do with it! I didn't go anywhere near it, I was so busy chopping wood!"

"I assure you that the goat is perfectly healthy except for a broken leg," urged its owner. "It's in fine condition, and you can roast half of it and keep the other half for a delicious stew the next day. Your family will enjoy several meals from this fine animal."

"I repeat," shouted the woodcutter, "I didn't even look in the direction of your flock, no less get close enough to hurt one of them! Go away, and stop bothering me, you ridiculous goatherd!"

When the goatherd realized that the woodcutter was in a snit, shouting at him without reason, he, too, became angry. Finally, he shouted back, "You ungrateful man! I am trying to provide a few meals for your family. What's with you that you are yelling at me and waving your arms as if preparing to attack me?"

They kept screaming at each other, both in bad temper.

An itinerant tradesman, passing by and hearing their loud voices, led his horse toward them up the hillside, curious to learn what the shouting was about. He dismounted and joined them on the slope to inquire into this violent argument.

Totally frustrated by now, the goatherd turned toward the tradesman and said as calmly as he could, "I am trying to give this man a gift because he was kind enough to look after my flock when I went back to the village to get my lunch. For some reason that I cannot fathom, he seems to take my gratitude as an insult, and keeps shouting at me and threatening me as if he would hit me. I am shouting back because I don't understand his anger at my offer of a generous gift."

The woodcutter, for his part, calmed down long enough to explain his point of view: "This vile goatherd dares to blame me because one of his animals broke its leg while I was chopping wood. I'm furious, and I'm telling him that I did not so much as look in the direction of his herd while he was gone, and certainly had nothing to do with the animal's accident."

The merchant cupped his hands over his ears, for, by a strange twist of fate, he also could not hear and he was certain that both men were accusing him of something he had done.

"Yes," he confessed, "you are right. This horse is not mine. I found him drinking at a brook up the road about a half mile from here. I looked for his owner, who was no-where to be found. Since the poor animal was obviously lost and I was extremely tired, I climbed on his back. I planned to return him to his master, who was sure to be nearby. Since the horse apparently belongs to you, please take him with my apologies."

As they stood there in utter confusion, who should pass by but a dervish, who could hear, Allah he praised! The three deaf men turned to him and begged him to deliver them from their weird predicament by hearing their stories and judging right from wrong.

Now, I must tell you that although the dervish could hear, he could not speak, since he was afflicted by dumb-ness so profound that not a word could come from his mouth. He looked at the three men as they recounted their versions of the incident to him, gazing at them steadily with his gleaming black eyes.

The goatherd, the woodcutter, and the tradesman were tired of all the shouting and arguing. The steady, unblinking gaze of the dervish calmed them down, but they became frightened of his effect on them. They feared that he had some mystical power, and had magically bewitched them to let go of their anger. What more could he do to them with his strange power?

The frightened tradesman, who had taken a horse that was not his, turned around and ran down the hill, leaving the animal behind.

The woodcutter quickly gathered all the fuel he had amassed and piled it into a net that he had spread out for this purpose. Hoisting the heavy load onto his back, he trudged off as fast as he could go, weighed down as he was.

The dervish stared at them as they departed, then turned and fixed his unblinking stare on the goatherd. Frightened of the glittering eyes that seemed to gaze through him, and unable to drive his flock home so early in the day, the goatherd did the only thing he could do to get away from the magical effect of the dervish's steady stare. He simply drove his goats higher up the slope of the hill, where the grass had not been eaten and they could graze to their hearts' content.

When they had all quietly departed, the dervish mounted the horse and went on his way, convinced that to a great extent the power of speech is one that human beings could do without. I find, after deep thought on this subject, that I concur with the dervish in this profound observation.

# A Kaleidoscope
of Human
Characteristics

# 36

# CLEVERNESS: THE UNBELIEVABLE LIE

Once Ibrahim, Commander of the Faithful, became bored and longed for entertainment that would divert him from his gloomy thoughts. He thought for a long while and finally came up with an amusing idea.

He sent for his most trusted courtiers and surprised them by saying, "Put on your thinking caps! I want each one of you to tell me a story that contains a lie I cannot possibly believe. Let's see how much imagination you have.

"If I find any reason to give credence to your tale, you will be thrown into the black mud of the river in your silken robes. If, on the other hand, you succeed in spinning a yarn that contains a lie I cannot possibly believe, you will receive as a reward a thousand gold dinars. I hope you'll find this idea as diverting as I do and that we will have some fun with it."

Daoud, the first of the courtiers, was clad in a silken robe of a beautiful blue hue adorned with magnificent embroidery. He came forward, bowed before Ibrahim, and launched directly into his tale:

"O Master! Last night after dinner, I entered my garden to have some fruit for dessert. On the ground among the watermelon plants, I found a huge green watermelon. I took out my knife and cut a deep slice.

"As I was enjoying the luscious fruit, my purse came loose from my belt and dropped into the hole I had made in the melon. I put my hand into the hole to retrieve my purse, but could not find it. I shoved my arm in up to my elbow, but still there was no purse.

"Amazed, I reached in up to my shoulder; still no purse. With my knife I enlarged the hole and thrust my head into it— still no purse. I carved away at the fruit and immersed myself in it up to my waist—again, no purse.

"Finally, I plunged right into the hole, clinging to the top edge of it with my toes. Suddenly, they slipped and I felt myself falling down, down, and down, past miles of pink fruit and thousands of black pits."

Commander Ibrahim interrupted. "I can believe that, because melons are slippery and when people fall they fall downward, not upward."

"But, Master, that is not all!" continued Daoud the courtier. "For I fell and fell and fell until I landed with a splash into a pond, unharmed. Imagine my astonishment when I realized that the pond was a drop of sweat on the brow of a sleeping giant.

"When the giant snored it was as if he unleashed a great gale. A strong gust of wind blew me from his brow into his hair. I wandered through this dense forest and saw fleas as big as horses. I mounted one of them and bounded over the top of the waving forest in great leaps.

"At the edge of the forest I found myself in an arid desert facing a stone castle in which a maiden was imprisoned. She cried out to me from high up in one of the turrets, 'Help! Help! Free me!'"

Again Ibrahim cut into the story. "That I can well believe, for imprisoned maidens often cry for help."

The courtier Daoud persisted, "But, Master! That is not all! To answer her appeal for assistance, I walked around the castle seven times, but could not find an entrance.

"What was I to do? I could not leave a lady in distress.

"I returned to the forest and cut a thousand hairs, each as tall as a date palm, too heavy for me to carry. To move the hairs to the tower, I harnessed them to the fleas the size of horses, you remember.

"I had the fleas pile the palms on top of each other end to end. This done, I was able to climb to the top of the tower, which was exactly a thousand palm trees high."

Ibrahim interrupted again. "That I can believe," he said, "for the height of all the hairs end to end must have equaled the height of the tower, since you reached the top of it."

The courtier Daoud persisted, "But, Master, that is not all! For as I entered the tower, the frightened maiden greeted me and told me of a lion that lived in that castle.

"I descended to the lowest depths of the castle, where I found a lion bigger than a thousand lions. You won't believe this, but it is true that this huge beast was weeping from pain because a camel was stuck in his eye!

"Full of sympathy, I removed the camel. Both animals thanked me effusively, and the three of us sat down to eat. The dish set before us was a roasted elephant, and in the stomach of the elephant was a bullock, and in the stomach of the bullock was a sheep, and in the stomach of the sheep was a chicken, and in the stomach of the chicken was my lost purse that had fallen into the watermelon."

And Ibrahim declared, "That I do believe, for you were looking for your purse and men frequently do find what they seek. Therefore your story is real and believable, and you shall be thrown into the mud."

As commanded by Ibrahim, his courtiers threw Daoud into the river. When he emerged, his silken blue embroidered robe was covered with the loathsome mud, as was his entire body from the top of his head to the bottom of his shoes.

Some of the other courtiers laughed and jeered, "Look at Daoud's ruined robe and his hair matted with mud!"

The wiser ones, however, whispered to each other, "We shall all have the same fate, for if Ibrahim could believe that pack of lies, won't he believe ours as well?"

Next Haroun, a courtier dressed in a silken robe the color of roses, addressed Ibrahim. "Listen to my story, Master, for you will find it hard to believe!

"Yesterday, I entered the bazaar with only one silver piaster. I saw a beautiful maiden dressed in silk and cloth of gold and adorned with pearls set in gold. I fell in love with her immediately, and to my surprise she returned the affection."

"That I can believe!" interrupted Ibrahim, "for people often experience love at first sight. Indeed, I believe that is the most enduring kind of love."

Haroun continued, "The problem was that I needed a house for her to live in. So with my piaster in my pocket I set out to find an appropriate house for such a beautiful maiden.

"I walked on until I came to a palace in the center of a gracious garden. It was just the kind of splendid, spacious home I wanted for my lovely maiden.

"I entered and found the owner hospitable and generous. After sharing a drink with him, I inquired, 'Would you agree to sell this palace?'

"The owner replied, 'I truly wish to sell it, for the walls are only silver and the floors are only marble, and the ceilings are only mosaics of gold and pearl. The great coffers in the storeroom are filled with only diamonds and rubies and topaz and amber and turquoise. I need a more splendid palace for my wives and family.'

"Encouraged, I inquired, 'What price are you asking for this humble abode then?'

"The owner responded, 'Since I really want to sell and since I can find no buyers, my price to you is half a piaster.'"

Ibrahim interjected, "That I can well believe, for when there are no buyers, the price falls."

"But, Master, that is not all! For I gave him my piaster, and he said, 'I will give you all new household supplies for the other half-piaster, since I have no change.'

"Again I believe you, because people in commerce often do not have change," interposed Ibrahim.

"He brought me a thousand horses and a thousand bags of ambergris and a cart load of peaches and a shipload of apricots and a thousand sheep and a boatload of walnuts and he said, 'There is a balance in your favor; please take my cloak to get your full value.'

"He took off his cloak of silk and gold cloth and gave it to me. When he departed, I put on the cloak and in the pocket I found the silver piaster that I had given him."

And Ibrahim said, "That I can well believe, for you gave him the piaster and he must have put it into his pocket where you found it. Therefore your story is true. Off you go to the river! To the river!"

Haroun the courtier in the rose-colored silk robe was seized and thrown into the mire. He was muddied from his toes to the top of his head, and neither he nor his beautiful robe could be distinguished from the river mud.

Then the courtier Jauher arose in his silken robe the color of persimmon embroidered in silk thread the color of corn. He saluted Ibrahim, the Commander of the Faithful, and said, "Master, listen to my story now, for I tell the truth and there is no lie in it:

"Last night, I lay down on my bed and fell asleep."

Ibrahim nodded his head and commented, "That I can well believe, because people do lie down on their beds to go to sleep."

The courtier Jauher went right on with his story, "I slept for an hour. Then I was wakened by a figure standing at my bedside wrapped in a shroud. I recognized the noble ancestor, your dead father, may Allah have mercy on him!

"Your dear dead father instructed me, 'Go to my son Ibrahim and give him a message from me. Tell him to bestow upon you a hundred thousand dinars in gold, for you are the worthiest man in his land. This is my wish and my command to him.'"

Ibrahim, Commander of the Faithful, remained silent, but his mind was active. He thought, "This is a lie that I cannot afford to believe."

Aloud, so that all his courtiers could hear, he proclaimed, "Jauher, you lie and I don't believe you! Now take this bag containing the reward I promised, a thousand gold dinars. You are spared the river because of your clever deception."

Jauher took the bag of gold with a smile. He thought to himself, "I have entertained my ruler with an interesting fabrication as he instructed. I have also served myself well by earning the money he promised to anyone who would use his intelligence to outwit him.

"I feel good on both counts. Now I will go home in my unsullied persimmon-colored robe and tell my story to my wife and children."

He bowed before Ibrahim, Commander of the Faithful, and thanked him in a loud voice. Then he turned and walked quickly in the direction of his home, where he would tell the story of this adventure to his family and bask in their admiration.

# 37

# FOOLISHNESS: A MEDLEY OF FOUR TALES

We Arabs also have our tales about human frailty and stupidity. When we tell about foolish people, we, too, hit out in all directions, as the Jews do when they tell about the people of Chelm. No one is safe from the barbs of the satire about stupidity.

Every person in the tale indulges in ridiculous ideas and actions except for the storyteller or the one person whose function in the story is to suffer the stupidity. Usually, the foolishness in such a tale rises in a crescendo, highlighting the harm that stupidity can wreak on people's lives. These tales are told with great fun and gusto.

An example is the story of one man's encounter with so much ridiculous thinking and behavior that it escalates beyond his tolerance, and he goes back to his simple wife whose foolishness is at least harmless to others. He finally finds comfort in her simplemindedness.

This is the story. I hope you like it:

Once upon a time there was a very simple woman called Khadijah, who always remained at home while her husband Izak was at work. He made sure of that, because he loved his wife very much, and he worried about the trouble she might get into if allowed to go wherever her silly mind would lead her. But Khadijah did not have to leave home for her foolishness to get her into trouble.

One day, while Khadijah was at home alone, a magician came through the streets of the town, crying out in a musical singsong, "New names for sale! New names for sale!"

Khadijah, in the middle of a daydream about flying over Arabia on a magic carpet while she baked her favorite honey cakes, nevertheless heard the magician's cry. She opened her window and called down to him, "Can you really sell me a new name? I am twenty-one years old and for at least twenty of those years, I've hated my name, Khadijah."

The magician looked up at her and responded in his gentle singsong voice, "And why should you suffer for twenty years more or even, if you are lucky and live a long time, as much as thirty or forty years more, hating your name? Give me one good reason you should suffer so much and so long when there is an easy remedy. I have many beautiful names for sale!"

Khadijah suddenly remembered that her husband always asked the price before he bought anything. "And how much do you charge for a new name?" she asked, furrowing her brow as she concentrated on being shrewd enough to strike a good bargain.

The magician responded speedily in his soft, persuasive voice, "I ask only a thousand piasters!"

That did not seem too much to Khadijah. "And may I choose any name I like?" she inquired.

"Indeed you may," answered the magician generously. "You may select any name from my long list: Jamine, Hanan, Sit Bdour, Kut-ul-kuloob, or any other."

"Then I shall choose the name Rose," Khadijah offered, smiling happily.

She ran to the chest in which her husband kept the money he had saved during years of hard work. She filled a bag with a thousand piasters and dropped it into the magician's eager, outstretched hands.

"Now my name is Rose!" she sighed happily. The magician departed from the simple woman. Both were content with the transaction.

When Izak, Khadijah's husband, came home that evening, he found the house door barred. He called out, "Khadijah!" There was no answer.

He shouted again, "Ho, Khadijah!"

Still no answer.

He raised his voice, thinking his wife must be asleep. Then he knocked at the door harder and harder. Growing anxious, he began to kick the door. At last he picked up a large stone, broke the door down, and entered his house.

To his amazement, he found his wife on a couch, smiling happily as though nothing had happened. Enraged, Izak called Khadijah names no man in his right mind would call his wife. "Stupid woman! Idiot! Why didn't you answer when I called? Why didn't you open the door for me?"

Khadijah replied calmly, "I would have done so if you had called me by my right name!"

"Your right name?" shouted her husband. "And what might your right name be?" he asked sarcastically. "I always thought it was Khadijah!"

"It used to be, but my name is Rose now," declared Khadijah serenely.

Then she told the unfortunate man how she had bought a new name from a magician for the thousand piasters Izak had toiled for years to save.

Izak's rage knew no bounds. I will not shock you with the terrible things he said in his fury. We all remember getting carried away and offending even a beloved person when we allow our anger to escalate beyond control.

In the end, he calmed down enough to declare, "I cannot bear your foolishness any longer. This is the parting of our ways, Khadijah. I am going out into the wide world. If I meet anyone more foolish than you, I shall come back to you; but unless I do, you need never expect to see me again!"

He packed some provisions in a bag, said good-bye to the weeping Khadijah, and set out on his journey.

Izak came to a village in the evening. Tired and unhappy, he sat by the community well to eat and rest. As he drank the cool well water, the village tradespeople, having closed their shops, crowded around him, interested in where he was headed.

"I'm going to the Land of Damnation!" he replied curtly, too disgruntled to be polite, for he did not want to be annoyed by their questions.

The tradespeople understood him to mean the land beyond the horizon, which they referred to as the Land of Damnation because so few of their soldiers ever came back after being sent there to fight rebels. The merchants spoke to him with great animation.

"Kind stranger," cried one merchant, "that is where my son went with our army, and I have never heard from him since! Will you do me a favor and take these gold pieces to him? His name is Moussa Tarodi."

A tradeswoman pleaded, "My dear brother has also gone to the Land of Damnation. Do a good deed and take these jewels to him. I hope he will sell them and use the money to come home! His name is Farouk Al Kouli."

Many of the storekeepers gave him something they valued, as a gift for a son, a husband, a brother, or a betrothed. The traveler took down all the names and put the gifts in his bag. He accepted their thanks and best wishes and hurried out of the village as fast as he could.

He was only a few miles away when the village field-workers returned home after a day's harvesting. They found the whole population in a state of great excitement.

When they learned of the obliging stranger on his way to the Land of Damnation loaded with gifts of all kinds, the field-workers were very upset. They told their suspicions to the tradespeople. They all gathered together to discuss how to retrieve the treasure the stranger had carried off.

They reasoned that the man could not have gone very far and that a horseman would soon overtake him. They agreed that one of them would mount a swift horse and pursue him.

Izak the traveler looked up and saw the horseman a

short distance away, drawing nearer at great speed. Realizing that the horseman was pursuing him, he quickly dug a hole in the roadside, buried the treasure, and sat down to wait.

The horseman reined in his steed, saluted Izak and asked, "Have you seen a man walking in this direction carrying a bag filled with gold and precious stones?"

"Indeed I have," answered Izak. "He passed me about an hour ago. By this time he must have reached the top of yonder hill.

"But it seems to me, worthy man, that you will never catch up with him riding horseback. You see, a horse has four legs. By the time it puts down one foot and picks up another four times, the man you want would be out of reach. If you get down off your horse and pursue him on foot, you will soon overtake him."

The horseman pondered for a moment and then decided, "There is wisdom in your words, stranger!"

He jumped off his horse and handed the reins to Izak, saying, "Please hold my horse for me while I pursue the man and bring him back with me!"

Now, Izak the traveler had a horse. He waited a few minutes until the man was out of sight. Then he dug up the bag of gold and jewels, swung himself into the saddle, and galloped away in a different direction toward a town whose lights were visible in the distance.

By the time he entered the gate, the town was suffused in the purple and orange light of dawn. Although it was very early in the morning, the people were on the streets in a state of great commotion.

One man lamented, "What a pity the bride's head must be chopped off!"

Another responded, "It's a shame that they will have to cut off the mare's legs, in any case!"

Izak the traveler, who could make nothing of these strange remarks, asked what was wrong, and the townsfolk told him.

It seems that a wedding was being celebrated. The bride, mounted on a thoroughbred mare, was riding to the bridegroom's house after an all-night revelry, as was the custom, when the procession came to a tunnel under a bridge. The tunnel roof was so low that the bride could not pass beneath it mounted on the mare, unless, indeed, either the bride's head or the mare's legs were cut off. No wonder everyone was weeping and lamenting!

"What if I can solve the problem for you without cutting off either the bride's head or the mare's legs?" asked the traveler.

"You are sure to be handsomely rewarded," everyone told him, "for the bride's father is the richest man in town."

They led Izak to the entrance of the tunnel. There stood the mare, with the beautiful bride on its back. A group of women stood nearby weeping. The men formed another group. All were trying to find some way out of the difficulty.

"Weep and worry no more!" cried Izak to the gloomy and helpless crowd. "In a few moments both the bride and the mare will be safely at the other end of the tunnel."

Then he drew his horse close to the bride's mount and whispered to her, "Pretty bride, bend your head."

The young woman lowered her head, and lo and behold, she rode through the tunnel without the slightest difficulty!

"Wonderful! Wonderful!" cried the astonished townsfolk, full of admiration for the ingenious stranger.

"Let us make him the mayor of our town!" shouted some.

"He is a wizard!" cried others.

But Izak did not wish to be the mayor of such a town, nor did he feel flattered by the admiration heaped upon him. He was pleased to be entertained with lavish hospitality and presented with a large sum of money by the bride's father.

The next day, Izak the traveler mounted his horse and rode to the next town, which he reached as evening shadows were falling and the dusk still had a rosy glow.

He asked for lodging. Following directions, he took shelter with a family consisting of a man, his wife, a son, and a daughter of marriageable age.

The traveler unsaddled his horse and asked for water for the tired animal. The woman turned to her daughter and said, "Hanan, go and fetch water from the well for our guest's horse!"

When Hanan the daughter arrived at the well, she lowered her water jar from her head and set it down so that she might rest for a moment. Relaxed, she looked deeply into the well and thought to herself, "This man has surely come to ask my parents for my hand in marriage. Soon he will marry me, we will set up housekeeping together, and in due time a son will be born to us.

"The boy will grow up strong and well, and then one day I shall send him to this very well to fetch water. But alas, he will look at his reflection in the water as I am doing. As he leans over to examine it, he will slip, fall into the well, and drown."

At once she began to cry, "Oh, my child, my child, why didn't your mother die instead of you?" Full of grief over her drowned son, she forgot all about her errand and remained at the well weeping.

When she did not return with the water, her parents wondered what could have happened to their daughter. They turned to their son and said, "Mokhmad, go to the well and see what is keeping your sister."

At the well, the young man found his sister wailing and lamenting, the tears streaming down her cheeks.

"Why are you crying, Hanan?" he asked. "And why do you linger here beside the well?"

Hanan looked up at her brother and questioned, "Hasn't the stranger in our house come to propose marriage to me?"

Mokhmad agreed that this might very well be the case. Hanan then told him of the tragedy her imagination had conjured up. When she came to the point where her son had fallen into the well and drowned, her brother began to lament with her and cried, "Oh, my nephew, why couldn't your uncle have died instead of you?"

The two wept bitterly while their parents waited anxiously for them at home.

Finally, the husband turned to his wife and said, "Perhaps you had better go and see what has become of our son and daughter at the well!"

The woman immediately hurried to the well, where she found Hanan and Mokhmad weeping and lamenting as though their hearts would break. Her daughter related the tale she had fantasized.

Soon her mother was crying as well. "Oh, my grandson, my grandson, why couldn't your grandmother have died in your stead?"

Then all three sat and wept.

Up at the house, after waiting patiently, the father of the family finally turned to Izak the traveler and said, "Make yourself comfortable here, while I go to the well to find out what this delay is all about!"

He found his wife, son, and daughter sitting at the well, weeping and lamenting loudly.

"What is the trouble?" he asked.

His wife told him their daughter's story, and soon the father, too, was weeping and calling out, "Oh, my grandson, my grandson, why couldn't your grandfather have died in your stead?"

Izak the traveler waited in vain for the people of the house to return. By now it was quite dark, and he began to fear that some misfortune had overtaken the entire family. He stepped out of the house and asked the people in the street to direct him to the town well. There he found the whole family gathered, weeping and lamenting.

When he asked the reason for their tears, his host repeated his daughter's story, adding, "Is it not so? Haven't you come to ask my daughter's hand in marriage?"

"Indeed I have not," Izak replied, surprised and outraged. "I am married already, and I might as well tell you that I am going back to my wife this very minute!"

With these words, he mounted his steed and rode back to his town, which he reached in three days.

When he arrived at his house, he knocked at the door

and shouted, "Open the door, Rose! I'm home, Rose, my wife!"

When she appeared in the doorway, he took her in his arms, embraced her closely, and whispered in her ear, "With all your simplicity you are wiser by far than any of the folk I have met in my travels!"

For many years thereafter, he mused about the foolishness he had encountered during his venture into the world, and wondered how widespread it really is. He also remembered his own dishonest behavior and wondered which was worse, the foolishness of the others or the shrewd dishonesty he had displayed.

# 38

# INTEGRITY: ITS SURVIVAL DESPITE MISFORTUNE

W e admire and treasure honesty and integrity. Yet these attributes are so very rare!

I want to tell you a true tale about the integrity of two men who encountered each other briefly but twice, each time under a different circumstance. Yet they would remember each other for the rest of their lives, each admiring the other's integrity. This is the unusual story:

Once there was a merchant named Mahoud, who had spent his money foolishly and became overwhelmed by debts. When he realized he had no resources even to put food on the table, he became so frightened of the future and what it would bring to his family, his wife and children, his old mother and father, that he could think of nothing else.

He knew that he should pull himself together and work hard to earn enough money to pay his debts and to provide his family with food and clothing. However, he had become so fearful of the future that he felt he would go mad if he stayed at home.

Believe it or not, he left his wife, his children, and his native village and became an itinerant beggar. He wandered around the world, scarcely knowing where he was, begging his way from place to place.

At last he came to a great city, whose name he did not recognize. He entered through the magnificent ironwork gates onto the main street and gazed around him in wonderment at the beautiful buildings, the shops, and the bazaars. Suddenly, a group of richly dressed men passed him, talking animatedly. Having nothing else to do, Mahoud followed behind them, trying to remain as inconspicuous as possible.

Before long, he found himself walking with them through an intricately carved marble doorway into a splendid palace. When they came to the great hall, he saw them bow low before a man who looked like a prince, for he was seated on a golden chair surrounded by attendants dressed in resplendent red livery.

Mahoud began to tremble because he was in rags and he knew he had no right to be there. He feared for his life if he were recognized as an uninvited guest.

He moved quickly to a dimly lit corner of the great hall. There he sat down on the marble floor and leaned against the wall to rest, relieved that no one seemed to take notice of him. They were all too busy eating delicious-looking food, which was served to them in golden bowls. There was a loud hum of conversation and every once in a while there would be a burst of song in a deep, melodious chorus of male voices.

Mahoud sat in his corner, weak and hungry. After a while, a gamekeeper entered, leading four gold-collared hunting dogs whom he tied with chains made of silver to a pole in a corner of the hall, not far from where Mahoud was crouching.

The servant set before each dog a large golden dish full of the choicest meats and vegetables. He then went away, leaving the dogs to their meals.

Poor Mahoud watched the dogs enviously as they ate. A few moments later, he noticed that one of the dogs had not touched his food and was staring at him. It seemed to see the hunger in Mahoud's face, for it drew back from its dish and gestured with its paw for Mahoud to come and eat. Mahoud ate the dog's food eagerly, smiling his gratitude to the animal.

When he had emptied the dish, Mahoud put it down on the floor in front of the dog, who pushed it back toward him, clearly indicating that he must take it. Mahoud picked up the golden dish and hid it under his rags. He ran out of the hall, feeling very much the thief.

Mahoud journeyed on until he came to another town, where he sold the dish for a thousand ducats of gold.

Joyously, he returned to his native village, to his wife and family, who had suffered greatly from poverty while he was away. Mahoud was able to pay all his debts, and set up in business again.

This time he prospered, for he had become very much wiser during his many months of travel. He accumulated more and more riches as the years went by.

The thought of the golden dish weighed heavily on his mind, however, until he could bear his guilt no longer. He put a thousand ducats of gold into a purse, took a bag of precious jewels and set out for the great city. He rode on a fine camel with ten richly dressed attendants accompanying him.

When he entered the city that had been so splendid, he found it sadly changed. The walls were in ruins; the great iron gates had fallen from their hinges. The main street was empty except for a few scraggly dogs sniffing for food in the garbage that lined the gutters.

After dismounting, he left his camel with one of his men and set out on foot to find the beautiful palace in which the dog had given him the golden dish. It was difficult to find because time had not been kind to this city, which was in shambles.

When he finally reached the site of the palace, he found the building in total collapse. The walls were shattered and the roof had caved in. There was dirt and refuse on the floors that had once been covered with deep, colorful carpets. The only person he saw was an old man, pale and haggard, sitting on the broken steps of the main doorway.

"Ho there!" called the merchant. "What has brought ruin

on this magnificent city? What have time and fortune done to the lord of this palace?"

"I was its lord," replied the old man. "I built it and lived in it like a sultan until time robbed me of everything I had. But who are you, and why do you ask?"

The now wealthy merchant Mahoud told his story. At the end, he paused. The two men sat in silence for a few minutes.

Mahoud resumed, "I owe you a great debt and would like to repay it. I owe everything, my good fortune, my happiness, the security of my family, to that dish of gold, which belonged to you. I have here with me a thousand ducats of gold, the sum I received for the dish when I sold it, as well as a gift for you of precious stones. I beg you to accept these two bags from me, so that I can repay my debt."

The old man, now in rags, rose to his feet, looking as princely as he had when the merchant first saw him many years before. "My friend," he responded, "I thank you with all my heart. But can I be so mean as to take back the price of a gift that a dog of mine generously gave you?"

He turned and walked slowly away, disappearing into the shadows cast by the ruins of his palace.

# 39

# FRIENDSHIP: LOYALTY TRANSCENDS DEATH

Once two friends, an ant and a flea, were warming themselves before an open fire in the woods. They were happy because they loved each other and enjoyed sitting side by side talking about old times.

The flea, like all fleas, was happiest when he was jumping. Feeling gay, he leaped as high as he could and landed in the fire, which consumed the poor creature.

The ant was distraught and stood looking at the fire that had destroyed her friend. She pulled at her hair and cried and cried for her dear companion, the flea, whom she missed very much.

Soon a crow flew overhead. She saw the ant wailing and mourning by the fire. "Why are you weeping?" asked the crow.

"I am mourning for my friend, the Prince of Jumpers, who leaped into the fire and was consumed."

When she heard this, the crow stopped circling above the fire and flew into a nearby palm tree. She started to sob and to molt her feathers.

"Why are you sobbing and molting your feathers?" asked the palm tree.

The crow responded, "I am molting my feathers because my friend the ant is mourning the Prince of Jumpers, who leaped into the fire and was consumed."

No sooner had the palm tree heard this than it began to shed its leaves in sorrow.

Soon a wolf came to rest in the shade of the palm tree. When he found the tree bare of leaves, the wolf inquired, "Why have you shed your leaves, palm tree? You no longer give shade to passersby who seek relief in the heat of the day!"

"I have shed my leaves sorrowing for my friend the crow who molted her feathers because the ant is mourning the Prince of Jumpers, who leaped into the fire and was destroyed!"

When the wolf heard this, he began to howl in grief and shed his fur. Dry-mouthed from sobbing, he went down to the river to drink from its cool water.

When the river saw that the wolf had shed his fur, it asked, "Why have you shed your fur, wolf?"

The wolf responded, "I have shed my fur grieving with my friend the palm tree, who shed its leaves sorrowing for the crow, who molted her feathers because the ant is mourning her friend the Prince of Jumpers, who leaped into the fire and was consumed."

When the river heard this, it began to run dry. Before long, the shepherd Mahmoud came to the river bank to water his goats. The riverbed was dry!

Mahmoud questioned the river, "Why have your waters dried up?"

And the river answered, "My waters have run dry in sympathy for the wolf, who shed his fur grieving for the palm tree, which shed its leaves sorrowing for the crow, who molted her feathers because the ant is mourning the Prince of Jumpers, who leaped into the fire and was consumed."

Then the shepherd Mahmoud plucked the horns from the head of one of his goats and stuck them on his own head as a sign of mourning.

When his sister came to bring him his lunch, she asked, "Why do you go horned, Mahmoud? Are horns not the symbol of bereavement?"

Her brother replied, "I go horned weeping for my friend the river, which ran dry in sympathy for the wolf, who shed his fur grieving for the palm tree, which shed its leaves sorrowing for the crow, who molted her feathers because the ant is mourning her friend the Prince of Jumpers, who leaped into the fire and was consumed."

The shepherd Mahmoud's sister tore her clothes as a symbol of mourning.

When she came home, her mother asked, "Why have you torn your clothes, my daughter?"

"I have torn my clothes in support of my brother, who goes horned weeping for the river, which ran dry in sympathy for the wolf, who shed his fur grieving for the palm tree, which shed its leaves sorrowing for the crow, who molted her feathers because the ant is mourning for her friend the Prince of Jumpers, who leaped into the fire and was consumed."

The mother at once covered one eye with a patch so that she looked one-eyed.

When her husband, Abu Mahmoud, came home, he was astonished and cried out, "Why have you become one-eyed, my wife?"

He was astonished at her reply: "I have become one-eyed in sadness for my daughter, who has torn her clothes in support of her brother, Mahmoud, who goes horned weeping for the river, which ran dry in sympathy for the wolf, who shed his fur grieving for the palm tree, which shed its leaves sorrowing for the crow, who molted her feathers because the ant is mourning her friend the Prince of Jumpers, who leaped into the fire and was consumed."

The shepherd Abu Mahmoud at once took an awl and stuck it into the palm of his hand, wounding it.

At that moment, a young student happened to pass by. He stopped Abu Mahmoud from driving the awl further by asking, "Why are you piercing the palm of your hand with an awl?"

Abu Mahmoud replied, "I pierce the palm of my hand with an awl because I am heartbroken for my wife, who walks one-eyed in sadness for our daughter, who has torn her clothes in support of her brother, Mahmoud, who goes horned weeping for the river, which ran dry in sympathy for the wolf, who shed his fur grieving for the palm tree, which shed its leaves sorrowing for the crow, who molted her feathers because the ant is mourning her friend the Prince of Jumpers, who leaped into the fire and was consumed."

The young student took Abu Mahmoud by the arm and urged, "Come along with me, Abu Mahmoud, come along with me to the goat pen! There from the fleas on the goats, you will gather as many jumper princes as you wish. Otherwise, the whole world will weep and wail and go into mourning because a flea leaped into a fire and was consumed!"

Abu Mahmoud took the patch off his wife's eye and called to their son, Mahmoud, who took off the horns of sorrow and called to his sister, who mended her torn dress. All four went back to their work.

The river gushed water from its source and wound down the riverbed. The wolf's fur grew thick again. The palm tree sprouted new leaves. The crow grew new feathers.

The ant remained sitting alone by the fire, weeping for her friend the flea, the Prince of Jumpers, who had leaped into the fire and could no longer be her friend. No other flea could take his place.

# 40

# WILINESS AND CRUELTY: SON OF ADAM OUTWITS ANIMALS

Once there was a beautiful young Goose who lived by herself near a lake in the middle of a deep forest. She knew nothing of the great outside world. She found delicious herbs and grasses to eat, drank clear water from her spring-fed lake, and enjoyed the warmth of the sun, which shone on her. She was happy as she walked along the water's edge, calling out with an occasional "onk" to express her enjoyment of life.

Then one night she was frightened by a terrible dream. A tall, strange creature unlike any she had ever seen before, who walked on its hind legs, appeared before her and in a soft voice said, "I am Man, son of Adam. Come to me, little Goose, and let me stroke your soft feathers. They are so beautiful."

Pleased by this flattery, Goose approached the creature.

At that moment in her dream, she heard a deafening peal of thunder and a deep voice bellowed, "Beware the son of Adam! Little Goose, beware! Today he will be your friend; tomorrow he will kill you and eat you. He is the most cunning of creatures. He brings down the birds of the air with pellets of clay. In his nets he hauls fishes from the depths of the sea. With his wiles he can master the most powerful of beasts. Beware the son of Adam, beware, beware!"

Goose awoke but was afraid to emerge from the cover of her forest. Even when day came she remained hidden among the bushes and trees, until she became hungry and had to venture forth to look for food.

After a while she met a large handsome catlike animal, who greeted her pleasantly. "Who are you?" he asked.

"I am Goose, of the bird creatures," she answered. "And who, sir, are you?"

"I am Lion, son of the King of Beasts. But why do you look so frightened? I will not hurt you, beautiful Goose."

Then Goose told Lion her dream. He lashed his tail in fury and roared. The hills echoed and reechoed the deafening sound. Finally, he calmed down and growled in sympathy, "My father warned about the same peril. All the creatures on earth are in danger so long as the son of Adam lives."

"Prince Lion," pleaded Goose, "you are so strong and brave. You are our only hope. Find Man, the son of Adam, and kill him, I beg you, before he kills all of us!"

"I will do that, I promise!" declared Lion. "Even though he is cunning, I will outwit him!"

And Lion set out, Goose close beside him. Soon they came to a dusty road. As they walked along, they saw in the distance a cloud of brown dust moving toward them. A creature galloped out of the dust, panting and braying.

"Stop!" ordered Lion. "Who are you? Why are you running so fast?"

"I am Ass of the animal creatures, and I am fleeing from the son of Adam," answered the breathless donkey in his loud honking voice.

"Ur-rh," roared Lion. "Are you afraid that the son of Adam will kill you?"

"No, Prince Lion," explained Ass, "but he makes me his slave. He places a heavy object called a saddle on my back and binds it with thongs called girths, which he tightens under my belly. He thrusts a hard piece of iron into my mouth and fastens it with leather thongs. He climbs onto my back and stabs me with a sharp thing called a goad to make me carry him wherever he wants to go.

"This will go on year after year, until I am too old to carry him anymore. Then he will sell me to the water carrier, who will hang heavy skins of water across my back and make me walk through the streets with the heavy load until I die of exhaustion. Have you ever heard of such cruelty?"

Goose shivered with fear at the donkey's story and Lion roared again in anger.

Suddenly, another cloud of dust appeared on the road. Ass brayed in terror, flung up his heels, and galloped away.

"This may be the son of Adam," growled Lion, sharpening his long claws on the hard ground. Goose hid behind a bush, and they waited together.

Out of the dust cloud came a handsome black horse who had a blaze on his forehead the size of a bright silver dollar. Neighing loudly, he came to a halt before Lion and gracefully lowered his head in greeting.

"O majestic beast," Lion addressed him, "who are you and why are you fleeing toward the wilderness?"

"O Prince, I am Horse of the animal creatures, and I am fleeing from the son of Adam."

"Aren't you ashamed?" asked Lion. "You are a splendid beast, strong and swift of foot. Why, you could defeat son of Adam with a single kick of your hoof! Why do you run away?"

"Because I am no match for him, O Prince. He deceives me with his cunning ways. He ties me with ropes made of palm fibers to keep me from leaving him. He secures my head fast to a high peg so that I can neither kneel nor lie down. He places a saddle on my back. He thrusts an iron bit in my mouth and pulls it taut with leather thongs called reins. He mounts on my back and forces me to go wherever he wishes.

"When I grow too old to carry him swiftly, he will sell me to the miller, who will blindfold me and force me to walk around and around in a circle working his mill, until one day I'll fall down dead. Do you wonder that I flee from the son of Adam?"

Goose shivered with fear and Lion lashed his tail furiously. At that moment, they saw another cloud of dust approaching them on the road.

Horse looked terrified. "That must be the son of Adam," he neighed. "I won't let him make me his slave again!" And with a great flurry of thudding hoofs, he galloped away.

Out of the dust cloud came a strange gurgling sound. Lion crouched like a cat ready to spring on its prey. Soon, however, the tawny head of a camel rose above the dust. The great beast came to a halt beside Goose and Lion and stopped his angry gurgling.

"Greetings, Prince Lion!" he said. "Greetings, my fair young Goose!"

"Greetings, Camel!" responded Lion. "Why do you gallop so fast? Are you fleeing from the son of Adam?"

"Indeed I am," replied Camel. "All animals who hope to avoid being harmed by this dangerous creature must flee from him."

"But you are so big and capable," ventured Lion. "You surely are strong and fleet enough to render him harmless!"

"No," answered Camel. "He is too clever. No one can defeat him except Death. He puts a string of goat's hair through my nostrils and calls it a nose ring. Over my head he places a halter that grips me by the throat. He makes me helpless so that the smallest child can lead me around. Then he loads me with heavy burdens and makes me carry them across the desert. He works me day and night unmercifully.

"When I am too worn out to be of use to him, he will take me to the butcher, who will kill me. Son of Adam will then sell my hide to the tanner to make leather and my flesh to the cooks to make food for believers in Allah. There is no hope for me unless I escape as soon as possible."

"When did you leave the son of Adam?" asked Lion.

"At sunset yesterday," replied Camel. "I am sure he is following me. I have galloped all night and all day, and I am very tired. I dare not stop until I have found a hiding place where the son of Adam cannot find me."

"Wait!" cried Lion. "Wait here with us until he comes. Then you'll watch me tear him to pieces and you'll know that you're free."

"I don't dare," declared Camel. "I must go, Lion. The son of Adam may be too clever, even for you. And look, he's coming now!"

Another cloud of dust had appeared on the long, sandy road. Camel looked at it for a moment. Then he turned and galloped away toward a clump of dwarflike trees in the distance, where he would seek refuge.

Again Lion crouched, getting ready to spring. This time the cloud of dust was small and it moved slowly. When at last it reached them, what emerged from it was the funniest little creature they had ever seen. It was like an old monkey with a wrinkled face, and it walked or rather staggered along on its hind legs. It carried a basket of tools on one shoulder and on the other a dozen planks of wood.

Lion went to meet the funny little fellow and said kindly, "Greetings, little creature! Who are you and why do you come this way carrying such heavy burdens?"

"O Prince of Beasts," replied the queer little creature, "may the blessings of Allah be upon you! I am Carpenter of the Carpenter creatures, and . . . and . . ." He burst into tears. ". . . and I am fleeing from the son of Adam, who is my enemy."

"You are right to fear the son of Adam," Lion assured him, "since you are such a feeble creature. But where are you going? And why are you carrying all that wood?"

"O Prince," responded Carpenter, "your royal father's Wazir, the Lord Leopard, has sent for me to build him a strong fort as a shield against his enemies."

"It is not right," retorted Lion, "that Leopard should have a fort if I don't have one. You must build a fort for me with that wood here and now."

"No!" cried Carpenter, trembling. "I dare not! If Lord Leopard hears of it, he will kill me!"

"What!" roared Lion. "Will you disobey me?" He gave Carpenter a pat with his powerful paw.

It was a gentle pat, but Carpenter fell flat on his back in the dust, his tools and wooden planks on top of him in scattered disarray. Lion keeled over with laughter because Carpenter looked so silly, and even tense little Goose giggled.

Carpenter was angry, but he was afraid of Lion. He pretended to smile and staggered to his feet, shaking the dust off his clothes.

"Now," bellowed Lion, "will you build me a fort?"

"I will, Your Royal Highness," groveled Carpenter.

He got to work at once with saw and hammer and nails, and soon completed a little house with small square holes for windows and a miniature door. He turned to Lion and bowed, pointing to his work and looking for approval.

Lion walked around the fort, looking at it doubtfully. "It is small," he remarked.

"But very strong," offered Carpenter. "Will Your Highness deign to enter it to see if it's the right size for you?"

Lion squeezed himself through the narrow doorway, but the house was so small that his tail was left outside. Carpenter twisted the tail and jammed it into the boxlike fort. He slammed the door and with a dozen blows of his hammer nailed it fast.

There came a muffled roar from Lion. "Let me out, Carpenter, let me out, or you'll suffer for this!"

"Not I!" shouted Carpenter, dancing for joy. "Make fun of me, will you? Knock me down, will you? Laugh at me, will you? I am Man, son of Adam! And I have the last laugh!"

He picked up his longest chisel and, pushing it through

one of the square windows, stabbed Lion to death. Then he shouldered his bag of tools and went back the way he had come, singing to himself.

Goose never stopped running until she was safe at home again on the shores of her lake in the dark forest, where she mourned the death of her friend Lion. She remained in the woods, avoiding all contact with Man, the son of Adam, for the rest of her life.

## About the Author

Now professor emeritus of Boston University, Blanche Serwer-Bernstein was formerly on the faculties of Harvard University, Queens College, and the City College of New York. Known for her work in learning disabilities and family therapy, she is a practicing psychologist who conducted multi-family groups in the Payne Whitney Clinic of Cornell Medical School.

A graduate of Barnard College and the Teachers' Institute of the Jewish Theological Seminary of America, she received her master's degree from the City College of New York and her Ph.D. from New York University. She was later trained as a psychodramatist at the Institute for Sociodrama. Professor Serwer-Bernstein is the author of *Let's Steal the Moon: Jewish Stories Ancient and Recent*, as well as research reports and articles in her fields of interest.